The Great US Presidential Elections 2024

The History, Stories and Surprises of U.S. Presidential Contests

PREFACE

The American presidency, a beacon of hope and power, has captivated the nation's imagination for centuries. From the crucible of the Revolutionary War to the complexities of the modern era, the pursuit of the highest office in the land has been a dynamic and ever-evolving spectacle. This book delves deep into the heart of this extraordinary process, offering a comprehensive exploration of the American presidential election.

We journey through time, from the formation of the Electoral College, a cornerstone of our democratic system, to the high-stakes campaigns that dominate our current political landscape. Along the way, we encounter iconic figures who shaped the nation's destiny, as well as lesser-known individuals whose stories are equally compelling. We examine the strategies, the triumphs, the setbacks, and the enduring allure of the presidency.

Beyond the familiar narratives of presidential elections, this book seeks to illuminate the intricate mechanics that underpin our democratic process. We explore the evolution of political parties, the impact of technology, the changing demographics of the electorate, and the role of media in shaping public opinion. By understanding these factors, we gain a deeper appreciation for the challenges and opportunities that face our nation.

Whether you are a seasoned political observer or a

curious newcomer to the world of elections, this book offers a rich and informative experience. It is our hope that by examining the past, we can gain valuable insights into the present and future of American democracy.

TABLE OF CONTENTS

Introduction: The Grand Spectacle
- The Allure of the Presidency
- America's Unique Election System

Part I: The Founding Fathers and the Electoral College
- Birth of a Nation: The Constitutional Convention
- The Electoral College: A Complex System
- The Early Presidents: Setting the Stage

Part II: The 19th Century: A Tale of Two Parties
- The Rise of Political Parties
- The Era of Jacksonian Democracy
- Civil War and Reconstruction
- Gilded Age and Progressive Era

Part III: The Roaring Twenties to the Great Depression
- The Jazz Age and Coolidge Prosperity
- The Great Depression and FDR's New Deal
- World War II and American Hegemony

Part IV: The Cold War and Civil Rights
- Truman, Eisenhower, and Containment

- Kennedy, Johnson, and the Turbulent 1960s
- Nixon, Watergate, and the Fall of a President
- Carter, Reagan, and the Conservative Resurgence

Part V: A New Era
- The First Bush Presidency and the End of the Cold War
- Clinton, Impeachment, and a Divided Nation
- George W. Bush, 9/11, and the Iraq War
- Obama, The First African American President

Part VI: The Trump Era and Beyond
- The Rise of Donald Trump
- The Trump Presidency: Policies and Controversies
- The 2020 Election and Beyond
- The Future of American Politics

Part VII: The Mechanics of an Election
- The Primary Process: Choosing Candidates
- Campaign Strategies and Tactics
- The Role of Media
- Election Night and Beyond

Conclusion: The Enduring Allure of the Presidency
- The Impact of Presidents
- Challenges and Opportunities for Future Leaders
- Engaging in the Political Process

Additional Chapters (Optional):
- Vice Presidents: The Unsung Heroes
- First Ladies: Influence from the White House
- Campaign Finance and Lobbying
- The Electoral Map: Swing States and Battlegrounds

- Third-Party Candidates: The Outsiders
- Voter Turnout and Demographics

INTRODUCTION

Every four years, the United States transforms into a nation gripped by a unique brand of fever. A fever fueled by ambition, rhetoric, and the promise of change. This is the quadrennial spectacle of a presidential election, a democratic drama unlike any other.

The presidency of the United States is more than just a job; it's a global spotlight, a mantle of power that can shape the course of nations. To occupy the Oval Office is to hold the fate of millions, if not billions, in your hands. The journey to this pinnacle is a gruelling, often brutal, contest that has captivated the world for centuries.

From the small town rallies to the billion-dollar ad campaigns, from the fiery debates to the nail-biting election night, the American presidential race is a rollercoaster of emotions, strategies, and unexpected twists. It's a battleground where ideologies clash, promises are made, and history is often rewritten.

This book is an invitation to step into the heart of this extraordinary spectacle. We will journey through time, from the nation's founding to the present day, to explore the triumphs and tribulations of those who sought, and often achieved, the highest office in the land. We will delve into the strategies, the scandals, the surprises, and the seismic shifts that have shaped America.

Prepare to be captivated by the drama, intrigued by the complexities, and inspired by the potential of a nation that puts its faith in the ballot box every four years. The story of American presidential elections is not just a tale of politics; it's a reflection of the American soul.

Part - I

THE FOUNDING FATHERS AND THE ELECTORAL COLLEGE

- Birth of a Nation: The Constitutional Convention
- The Electoral College: A Complex System
- The Early Presidents: Setting the Stage

Chapter - 1

BIRTH OF A NATION

A new nation was forged in the furnace of the American Revolution. But forming a government was as difficult a task as winning the war. The Constitutional Convention of 1787 was a gathering of extraordinary minds tasked with an impossible task: to craft a blueprint for a nation that would balance liberty with order, power with moderation. Philadelphia was a hotbed of ideas in the summer of 1787. Fifty-five delegates, including politicians, lawyers, and planters, came together with a shared vision of a united America, yet were deeply divided over how to achieve it. One of the most important questions was the nature of the executive power. Should it be strong or weak? How would it be chosen? And what checks would be placed on its authority? The convention was a battleground of ideologies. The Federalists, led by Alexander Hamilton, advocated a strong central government with a powerful executive. The Anti-Federalists, wary of unchecked authority, advocated a weak presidency. The debates were fierce, often acrimonious, but ultimately constructive. The result was a series of compromises that shaped the American presidency for centuries. The Federalist Papers, a collection of essays written by Alexander Hamilton, James Madison, and John Jay, was a powerful defense of the Constitution, including the presidency. They argued for a strong executive to protect national security, economic prosperity, and individual rights.

As the convention began to end, an outline for the presidency began to take shape. The office would be filled by a person who would be indirectly elected by the people through an Electoral College. The president would be the commander-in-chief of the armed forces, the nation's chief executive, and the nation's chief diplomat.

Chapter - 2

THE ELECTORAL COLLEGE

The Electoral College, a unique system that has been in place for centuries, is at the heart of US presidential elections. It is a system that is often misunderstood, criticized, and defended with equal zeal. To truly understand the dynamics of American politics, it is necessary to understand how this complex process works.

At its core, the Electoral College is a system of indirect election. When voters cast their vote for a presidential candidate, they are actually voting for a group of electors committed to that candidate. These electors, usually party loyalists, formally elect the president.

The number of electors each state has is equal to the total number of its senators and representatives in Congress. This means that larger states have more electoral votes, giving them more weight in presidential elections. To win the presidency, a candidate must win a majority of electoral votes, which is currently 270.

The Electoral College was designed as a compromise between those who wanted the president to be directly elected by the people and those who feared the tyranny of the majority. It was also seen as a way to give smaller states a greater voice in the electoral process.

Over the years, the Electoral College has been the subject of intense debate. Critics argue that it can distort the popular vote, allowing a candidate to win the presidency without winning the most popular votes. They point to elections where the winner of the popular vote loses the Electoral College as evidence of the system's flaws.

Defenders of the Electoral College argue that it preserves the federal system by giving smaller states a greater say in the election. They also argue that it encourages candidates to campaign in a wide range of states rather than focusing only on populous areas.

Regardless of one's opinions on the Electoral College, it remains a fundamental part of the American political landscape. To understand the complexities of presidential elections it is necessary to understand its history, mechanism, and the controversies surrounding it.

But, importantly, the Constitution also established a system of checks and balances to prevent the presidency from becoming too powerful.

The birth of the presidency was a complex and often controversial process. The framers of the Constitution walked a difficult path, balancing the need for a strong executive and the fear of tyranny. The decisions they made had a profound impact on the country's future.

Chapter - 3

THE EARLY PRESIDENTS

The first occupants of the Oval Office were pioneers, sailing into uncharted waters. Their actions shaped the presidency for generations to come. George Washington, the revered general, was the reluctant first president. His decision to step down after two terms set a precedent that would be followed for more than a century, establishing a norm of civilian control over the military. Washington's presidency was characterized by a focus on nation-building. He laid the foundations of the federal government, appointed qualified officials, and guided the young nation through economic and foreign policy challenges.

His dignified demeanor and unwavering commitment to the Constitution solidified the presidency as an institution of respect and authority. Washington's vice president, John Adams, succeeded him in a politically charged atmosphere. A strong Federalist, Adams faced opposition from the emerging Democratic-Republican Party led by Thomas

Jefferson. His presidency was characterized by foreign policy crises, especially with France, and internal political divisions. Despite his intelligence and dedication, Adams' one term was not very successful.

Thomas Jefferson, a supporter of individual liberty and states' rights, adopted a different style for the presidency. His election in 1800 marked a peaceful transfer of power, a testament to the young nation's democratic processes. Jefferson reduced the size of government, cut taxes, and expanded westward. His purchase of the Louisiana Territory doubled the size of the nation, a bold move that shaped the country's destiny.

The early years of the presidency laid the groundwork for the institution that would evolve over time. The challenges faced by Washington, Adams, and Jefferson shaped the office and set expectations for future presidents. These early leaders, while different in their approaches, contributed to the development of the presidency as a cornerstone of American democracy.

Part - 3

19TH CENTURY

- The Rise of Political Parties
- The Era of Jacksonian Democracy
- Civil War and Reconstruction
- Gilded Age and Progressive Era

Chapter - 4

THE RISE OF POLITICAL PARTIES

The early years of the Republic were marked by a sense of unity forged in the furnace of revolution. However, as the nation began to grow and prosper, differing visions of the future began to emerge, leading to the formation of political parties. These organizations, which were initially informal factions, soon became powerful forces shaping the nation's destiny. The Federalist Party, led by the charismatic Alexander Hamilton, advocated a strong central government. They believed in a strong economy based on manufacturing and trade, and advocated close ties with Britain. Hamilton envisioned a nation where the federal government would play a key role in promoting economic growth and infrastructure development. The Federalists drew support from merchants, bankers, and industrialists who stood to benefit from their policies. In opposition to the Federalists stood the Democratic-Republican Party, led by Thomas Jefferson and James Madison. This party emphasized states' rights, agricultural interests, and the limited role of the federal government. Jefferson and his followers envisioned a nation of independent farmers who were wary of centralized power and the potential for tyranny. The Democratic-Republicans found support among farmers, small landowners, and those who feared the concentration of power in the hands of wealthy elites.

The rivalry between the Federalists and Democratic-Republicans transformed the political landscape, leading to heated debates over economic policy, foreign relations, and the proper role of government. Elections became fiercely competitive affairs, as each party sought to win the hearts and minds of voters. While the two-party system would evolve over time, the foundation laid by the Federalists and Democratic-Republicans continues to shape American politics today.

Chapter - 5

THE ERA OF JACKSONIAN DEMOCRACY

Charismatic military hero Andrew Jackson ushered in a new era of American politics. His presidency marked a dramatic departure from the aristocratic politics of the Founding Fathers. Jackson embodied the spirit of the common man, and his election signaled a shift in power from the established elite to the growing democratic masses.

Jacksonian democracy was characterized by a fervent belief in popular sovereignty and expanded suffrage. The era saw a significant expansion of the electorate, as property qualifications for voting were gradually eliminated. This expansion of political participation strengthened the democratic process, but also led to new challenges and complications.

During the Jacksonian era the spoils system, the practice of rewarding political supporters with government jobs, took root. While this system energized the party's base, it also bred corruption and inefficiency. Jackson's controversial veto of the Bank of the United States marked a significant assertion of presidential power and a victory for states' rights advocates.

However, the Jacksonian era was not without its contradictions. While it supported the common man, it also perpetuated inequalities, especially for Native Americans and African Americans. The forced removal of Native American tribes from their ancestral lands, known as the Trail of Tears, is a dark chapter in American history.

Despite its flaws, the Jacksonian era left a lasting legacy. It expanded political participation, strengthened the presidency, and laid the foundation for the modern American political system. The populist fervor unleashed by Jackson would continue to shape the nation for decades to come.

Chapter - 6

CIVIL WAR AND RECONSTRUCTION

Decades of regional tensions erupted into the Civil War, a devastating conflict that tested the nation's foundations. The presidency was thrust into a pivotal role, leading the nation through a period of unprecedented crisis and change. Abraham Lincoln, a man of deep faith and moral courage, assumed the presidency on the brink of the Civil War. His leadership during the conflict played a key role in preserving the Union.

Lincoln's Emancipation Proclamation, initially a military strategy, became a moral beacon that set the stage for the abolition of slavery. His assassination, a tragic loss to the nation, left a void in leadership as the country embarked on the difficult task of Reconstruction. Lincoln's successor, Andrew Johnson, faced the difficult challenge of rebuilding the nation. However, his liberal Reconstruction policies proved inadequate, leading to political gridlock and the rise of Radical Republicans in Congress. Johnson's impeachment, though unsuccessful, exposed deep divisions within the nation over the future of the South. War hero Ulysses S. Grant succeeded Johnson as president. His administration was marked by considerable corruption, as scandals roiled his cabinet. Despite these challenges, Grant's presidency saw the passage of important civil rights legislation, including the Fourteenth and Fifteenth Amendments, which granted citizenship and suffrage to African Americans. However, implementation of these laws was met with fierce resistance in the South, leading to a period of violence and oppression known as Reconstruction. The Civil War and Reconstruction era was a time of intense upheaval and change. The nation was irrevocably changed, and the presidency emerged from this crisis as a more powerful and influential institution. The challenges and successes of this period continue to shape American politics and society today.

chapter - 7

GILDED AGE AND PROGRESSIVE ERA

The late 19th century was a period of unprecedented economic growth and industrialization, often known as the Gilded Age. The nation saw the rise of powerful industrial giants, the expansion of railroads, and the growth of cities. Yet, this era of prosperity also saw gross inequality, political corruption, and social unrest. Gilded Age presidents often struggled to address the era's challenges. While some, such as Grover Cleveland, attempted to reform the spoils system and lower tariffs, their efforts were often hampered by political opposition and the influence of powerful corporate interests.

The presidency faded due to the immense power wielded by industrial giants. In response to the growing problems of the Gilded Age, a progressive movement emerged, which sought reforms in politics, economics, and society.

Progressives sought to break up monopolies, regulate big business, protect consumers, and improve working conditions. Women's suffrage, conservation, and urban reform were also major issues. The early 20th century saw the rise of progressive presidents such as Theodore Roosevelt and Woodrow Wilson. Roosevelt, a dynamic and charismatic leader, pursued many progressive reforms, including trust-busting, conservation, and consumer protection. Wilson, a scholar-politician, supported economic reform, antitrust legislation, and internationalism.

The Progressive Era marked a turning point in American politics, as the government began to take a more active role in addressing social and economic problems. Although the era did not fully resolve the nation's challenges, it laid the groundwork for the New Deal reforms that followed.

Part - 3

THE ROARING TWENTIES TO THE GREAT DEPRESSION

- The Jazz Age and Coolidge Prosperity
- The Great Depression and FDR's New Deal
- World War II and American Hegemony

Chapter - 8

THE JAZZ AGE AND COOLIDGE PROSPERITY

The 1920s, often painted in vibrant colors of optimism and exuberance, was a period of profound change for the United States. The nation, emerging from the shadow of World War I, embraced the spirit of modernity and consumerism. Jazz music, with its syncopated rhythms and infectious energy, captured the essence of the era, sparking a cultural revolution that challenged traditional values. President Calvin Coolidge, a man of few words, embodied the spirit of the times. His administration championed a hands-free approach to the economy, allowing businesses to flourish with minimal government interference. Fueled by easy credit and speculative mania, the roaring stock market became a symbol of American prosperity. Automobiles, once luxury items, became commonplace, reshaping cities and suburbs.

The decade saw an emerging consumer culture, as Americans embraced new technologies and products. Radio broadcasting connected the nation, while Hollywood movies offered escapism and entertainment. The rise of advertising created demand for goods, which fueled economic growth. However, cracks were beginning to appear beneath the surface of this apparent prosperity.

The gap between rich and poor widened, and many Americans were left out of the economic boom. The agricultural sector faced challenges, and the volatile growth of the stock market caused concern among some economists. These underlying issues would ultimately contribute to the catastrophic economic collapse of the 1930s.

Chapter - 9

THE GREAT DEPRESSION AND FDR'S NEW DEAL

The stock market crash of 1929 marked the beginning of a catastrophic economic downturn that later became known as the Great Depression. The illusion of prosperity was shattered as banks failed, businesses closed, and millions lost their jobs. The nation sank into a deep economic abyss, marked by widespread suffering and despair. Franklin D. Roosevelt, elected president in 1932, promised a "New Deal" to address the nation's crisis. His administration initiated an ambitious program of economic and social reform that was unprecedented in its scope and ambition.

The New Deal aimed to provide relief to suffering, recover the economy, and reform the financial system to prevent future crises. Several programs were implemented, including the Civilian Conservation Corps (CCC), which provided jobs for young men in conservation projects; the Works Progress Administration (WPA), which created jobs in public works projects; and the Agricultural Adjustment Act (AAA), which aimed to stabilize agricultural prices.

The Social Security Act established a system of old-age pensions and unemployment insurance, laying the foundation for the modern welfare state. Although the New Deal did not completely end the Great Depression, it did provide a ray of relief and hope. It expanded the federal government's role in the economy, and many of its programs endure as pillars of the American social safety net. However, the New Deal also faced criticism, with some arguing that it did not do enough, while others argued that it represented an excessive intrusion into the free market.

Chapter - 10

WORLD WAR II AND THE RISE OF AMERICAN HEGEMONY

The attack on Pearl Harbor in December 1941 pushed the United States into World War II. The nation mobilized its vast resources, transforming from a peacetime economy into a wartime power. The war years brought enormous sacrifice but also created a sense of national unity. President Franklin D. Roosevelt led the nation through the dark days of the war. His leadership, combined with the United States' unparalleled industrial might, ultimately played a key role in the Allied victory.

The war years also saw the emergence of a new generation of leaders who shaped the postwar world. The defeat of Germany and Japan elevated the United States to global superpower status. The nation emerged from the war with an unrivaled economic and military might.

The development of the atomic bomb further solidified America's position as a world leader. The war also accelerated social and cultural changes. Women entered the workforce in unprecedented numbers, challenging traditional gender roles.

The experiences of African American soldiers fighting for a nation that denied them equal rights at home fueled the civil rights movement. As the war drew to a close, the world faced a new reality. The old order had collapsed, and a new global order was emerging. The United States along with the Soviet Union emerged as the two major superpowers, setting the stage for the Cold War.

Part - 4

THE COLD WAR AND CIVIL RIGHTS

- Truman, Eisenhower, and Containment
- Kennedy, Johnson, and the Turbulent 1960s
- Nixon, Watergate, and the Fall of a President
- Carter, Reagan, and the Conservative Resurgence

chapter -11

TRUMAN, EISENHOWER, AND THE CONTAINMENT OF COMMUNISM

The end of World War II ushered in a new era of global politics, marked by a clear ideological divide between the United States and the Soviet Union. This Cold War, a period of constant tension and rivalry, would shape domestic and foreign policy for decades to come. President Harry Truman inherited a nation that stood at a crossroads. The task of transitioning from a wartime economy to peacetime presented enormous challenges.

However, the specter of communism loomed large.

Truman's response was the Truman Doctrine, a policy of containment aimed at preventing the spread of Soviet influence. The Marshall Plan, a massive economic aid package for war-torn Europe, was another major component of this strategy. Domestically, Truman faced a number of issues, including labor unrest and the growing momentum of the civil rights movement. His decision to desegregate the armed forces was a historic move, but it did little to quell growing demands for racial equality.

Popular war hero Dwight Eisenhower succeeded Truman in 1952. His presidency was marked by a focus on economic growth and stability. The Eisenhower era, often characterized as a period of prosperity and conformity, also saw the escalation of the Cold War. The arms race intensified, and the threat of nuclear war cast a long shadow over the nation. Eisenhower's doctrine of "massive retaliation" emphasized the use of nuclear weapons as a deterrent to Soviet aggression. While this policy contributed to a sense of security, it also heightened tensions and raised the risk of global catastrophe.

The Cold War, with its emphasis on national security and anti-communism, often overshadowed domestic issues. Still, the seeds of social change were being sown, and the Civil Rights Movement was gaining momentum. The decade would end with the nation at a crossroads, facing both the challenges of the Cold War and the demands of racial justice.

Chapter - 12

KENNEDY, JOHNSON, AND THE TURBULENT 1960S

The 1960s were a decade of intense social and political upheaval. A new generation, excited by the promise of progress and inspired by a spirit of idealism, challenged the status quo. The presidency found itself at the center of these tumultuous times, grappling with crises both domestic and international.

John F. Kennedy, the youngest elected president in history, brought a sense of youthful optimism to the White House. His inaugural address, with its call to national service, inspired a generation. Kennedy's administration launched a number of ambitious programs, including the space race and the Alliance for

Progress. The Cuban Missile Crisis, a tense standoff with the Soviet Union that brought the world to the brink of nuclear war, underscored the fragility of peace in the Cold War era.

Kennedy's assassination in 1963 shocked the nation and the world. His successor, Lyndon B. Johnson, sought to carry on Kennedy's legacy. The Great Society, a sweeping set of domestic programs, aimed to eradicate poverty, improve education, and expand civil rights. Programs such as Medicare and Medicaid expanded the social safety net, while the Voting Rights Act of 1965 marked an important milestone in the struggle for racial equality.

However, the 1960s were also a decade of disillusionment and division. The Vietnam War, a growing quagmire, eroded public confidence in government and fueled anti-war protests. The assassination of Martin Luther King Jr. in 1968 sparked urban riots and heightened racial tensions. The decade ended with the nation deeply divided and uncertain about the future.

Chapter - 13

NIXON, WATERGATE, AND THE FALL OF A PRESIDENT

Richard Nixon, a seasoned politician with a reputation for shrewdness, won the presidency in 1968 by promising to restore law and order. His foreign policy initiatives proved to be some of his greatest achievements. De-escalation with the Soviet Union and openness with China marked a significant shift in American diplomacy.

However, Nixon's legacy was forever tarnished by the Watergate scandal. In 1972, a burglary at the Democratic National Committee's headquarters in the Watergate complex exposed a web of political espionage and cover-ups hatched by Nixon's campaign staff. The ensuing investigation revealed a pattern of abuse of power and obstruction of justice.

As the scandal deepened, public trust in the presidency eroded. Nixon, who was initially defiant, eventually faced impeachment proceedings. In a dramatic move, he resigned from office in 1974, becoming the first president to do so. The Watergate scandal had a profound effect on American politics. It led to reforms aimed at increasing government transparency and accountability. Public disillusionment with the government also fueled growing disappointment and distrust toward political institutions.

Chapter - 14

CARTER, REAGAN, AND THE CONSERVATIVE RESURGENCE

Former Georgia governor Jimmy Carter brought a sense of optimism toward outsiders to the White House. His presidency was marked by a commitment to human rights and a focus on domestic issues. However, a series of crises, including the energy crisis and the Iranian hostage crisis, eroded public confidence.

Ronald Reagan, a charismatic conservative, took advantage of the nation's discontent. His election in 1980 ushered in a new era of conservative politics. Reagan's economic policies, known as Reaganomics, emphasized tax cuts, deregulation, and reduced government spending. While these policies promoted economic growth, they also increased income inequality.

Reagan's foreign policy was marked by a staunch anti-communism stance. His rhetoric and policies contributed to the collapse of the Soviet Union. The end of the Cold War was a defining moment of the era, but it also presented new challenges for American foreign policy.

The Reagan years saw a resurgence of conservative values, focusing on personal responsibility and limited government. The Religious Right emerged as a powerful political force, influencing policy on issues such as abortion and school prayer. The legacies of the Carter and Reagan presidents are complex. Carter's emphasis on human rights and his commitment to public service have been praised, while his economic policies have been criticized. Reagan's economic policies remain a subject of debate, with supporters crediting him with reviving the economy while opponents argue that his policies increased inequality.

Part 5

A NEW ERA

- The First Bush Presidency and the End of the Cold War
- Clinton, Impeachment, and a Divided Nation
- George W. Bush, 9/11, and the Iraq War
- Obama, The First African American President

Chapter - 15

THE FIRST BUSH PRESIDENCY AND THE END OF THE COLD WAR

The presidency of George H. W. Bush marked an important transition period in American history, characterized by the end of the Cold War and the beginning of a new global order. When Bush took office in January 1989, the world was on the cusp of major changes, and his administration would go through some of the most important moments of the second half of the 20th century.

Republican George H. W. Bush was elected as the 41st president of the United States in 1988, succeeding Ronald Reagan, under whom he had served as vice president. Bush's extensive experience in public service, including roles as a member of Congress, ambassador to the United

Nations, and director of the CIA, established him as an experienced leader prepared to tackle the complexities of the international stage. The Fall of the Berlin Wall and German Unification One of the defining moments of Bush's presidency was the fall of the Berlin Wall in November 1989. The collapse of this symbol of communist oppression marked the beginning of the end of the Cold War.

Bush's diplomatic approach, characterized by caution and pragmatism, helped bring about the peaceful reunification of Germany in 1990. He worked closely with Soviet leader Mikhail Gorbachev and West German Chancellor Helmut Kohl to ensure a smooth transition that avoided conflict and maintained stability in Europe.

Dissolution of the Soviet Union

The dissolution of the Soviet Union in December 1991 was another important milestone during Bush's presidency. The end of the USSR effectively marked the conclusion of the Cold War era, ushering in a new geopolitical landscape. Bush's administration managed this transition while focusing on maintaining international order and supporting the emergence of independent, democratic states from the former Soviet republics.

Operation Desert Storm

In addition to these diplomatic accomplishments, Bush's presidency was marked by military action in the Middle East. In August 1990, Iraqi forces led by President Saddam Hussein invaded Kuwait, prompting a swift international reaction. Under Bush's leadership, the United States led a coalition of 35 nations in Operation Desert Storm, which liberated Kuwait in early 1991. The success of this operation solidified Bush's reputation as a decisive leader, able to mobilize international support for a just cause.

Domestic Challenges and Economic Recession

While Bush's foreign policy successes were significant, his administration faced challenges on the domestic front. The early 1990s saw an economic recession, which led to rising unemployment and a growing budget deficit. Despite his famous campaign pledge of "no new taxes," Bush's decision to raise taxes alienated many conservative supporters and contributed to his declining popularity.

Despite losing the 1992 presidential election to Democrat Bill Clinton, George H. W. Bush's presidency left a lasting legacy. His prudent handling of the end of the Cold War, commitment to international diplomacy, and leadership during Operation Desert Storm are remembered as high points of his tenure. Bush's presidency ushered in a new era in American foreign policy, with a greater focus on unipolarity and global cooperation.

Chapter - 16

CLINTON, IMPEACHMENT, AND A DIVIDED NATION

The presidency of William Jefferson Clinton, often referred to as Bill Clinton, was a period of remarkable economic growth, significant political change, and intense partisan conflict. Serving from 1993 to 2001, Clinton's administration oversaw a time of peace and prosperity but also became embroiled in controversy and scandal, leading to his impeachment.

The 1992 Election and Inauguration

Bill Clinton, a Democrat and the Governor of Arkansas,

won the 1992 presidential election against incumbent President George H. W. Bush and independent candidate Ross Perot. Clinton's campaign capitalized on economic issues, famously encapsulating its strategy with the phrase "It's the economy, stupid." His victory marked a shift toward a more centrist Democratic Party, often referred to as the "New Democrats," who embraced a blend of liberal and conservative policies.

Economic Policies and Prosperity

Clinton's presidency is often remembered for the robust economic performance of the 1990s. His administration implemented several key economic policies, including the Omnibus Budget Reconciliation Act of 1993, which raised taxes on the wealthiest Americans and aimed to reduce the federal deficit. The North American Free Trade Agreement (NAFTA), signed in 1993, created a trilateral trade bloc between the United States, Canada, and Mexico, promoting increased trade and economic integration.

Under Clinton's leadership, the U.S. economy experienced significant growth, low unemployment, and a budget surplus by the end of his second term. The technology boom, driven by the rise of the internet and the dot-com industry, further fueled economic expansion.

Welfare Reform and Crime Bill

In addition to his economic policies, Clinton's domestic agenda included welfare reform and crime prevention. The Personal Responsibility and Work Opportunity Reconciliation Act of 1996 transformed the welfare system, imposing work requirements and time limits on assistance. While controversial, this legislation reflected Clinton's centrist approach and his commitment to addressing the public's concerns about welfare dependency.

The Violent Crime Control and Law Enforcement Act of 1994, commonly known as the Crime Bill, aimed to reduce crime through increased funding for law enforcement, tougher sentencing laws, and the introduction of community policing. Critics argued that the bill contributed to mass incarceration, particularly affecting minority communities, but it also played a role in the significant decline in crime rates during the 1990s.

Attempt To Reform Health Care

One of Clinton's major policy initiatives was a comprehensive health care reform effort, led by First Lady Hillary Rodham Clinton. The proposed plan sought to provide universal health coverage, but it faced strong opposition from Republicans and segments of the healthcare industry. Despite extensive efforts, the initiative ultimately failed to pass Congress, highlighting the challenges of achieving major health care reform in the United States.

Foreign Policy and Global Engagement

Clinton's foreign policy was characterized by a focus on globalization, international trade, and humanitarian interventions. His administration played a key role in the peace process in Northern Ireland, the Balkans, and the Middle East. The Dayton Accords, brokered in 1995, ended the Bosnian War, while the Oslo Accords aimed to advance peace between Israel and the Palestinians, although a lasting resolution remained elusive.

The administration also faced challenges, including the rise of global terrorism. The 1993 World Trade Center bombing and the 1998 bombings of U.S. embassies in Africa underscored the growing threat of terrorism, which would become a more dominant issue in subsequent administrations.

Scandals and Impeachment

Clinton's presidency was marred by several scandals, the most significant of which was the Monica Lewinsky affair. In 1998, it was revealed that Clinton had engaged in an extramarital affair with Monica Lewinsky, a White House intern. The ensuing investigation led to charges of perjury and obstruction of justice, as Clinton denied the affair under oath.

In December 1998, the House of Representatives impeached Clinton, making him the second U.S. president to face impeachment. The Senate trial in early 1999 resulted in acquittal, as the charges failed to gain the necessary two-thirds majority for conviction. The impeachment process highlighted the deep partisan divisions within the country and had a lasting impact on American politics.

Despite the controversies, Clinton left office with high approval ratings and a legacy of economic prosperity. His presidency marked a shift toward centrist policies within the Democratic Party and demonstrated the potential for significant economic and social change. However, the scandals and impeachment underscored the complexities of personal conduct and public leadership, and the divisive nature of his presidency continued to influence American politics in the years that followed.

Chapter - 17

GEORGE W. BUSH, 9/11, AND THE IRAQ WAR

The presidency of George W. Bush, the 43rd President of the United States, was defined by significant events that reshaped American domestic and foreign policy. Serving from 2001 to 2009, Bush's time in office was dominated by the terrorist attacks of September 11, 2001, and the subsequent War on Terror, including the wars in Afghanistan and Iraq.

The 2000 Election and Inauguration

George W. Bush, the Republican Governor of Texas and son of former President George H. W. Bush won the 2000 presidential election in one of the closest and most contentious elections in U.S. history. The outcome hinged on the results in Florida, leading to a protracted legal battle that culminated in the Supreme Court's decision in Bush v. Gore, which effectively awarded the presidency to Bush. This narrow victory highlighted the deep political divisions within the country.

September 11, 2001: A Day of Infamy

On September 11, 2001, the United States experienced the deadliest terrorist attacks in its history. Al-Qaeda terrorists hijacked four commercial aeroplanes, crashing two into the World Trade Center towers in New York City and one into the Pentagon in Washington, D.C., while the fourth plane, United Flight 93, crashed into a field in Pennsylvania after passengers attempted to overpower the hijackers. The attacks resulted in nearly 3,000 deaths and had a profound impact on the nation.

The War on Terror

In response to the 9/11 attacks, President Bush declared a War on Terror, a global effort to combat terrorism and prevent future attacks. The first major military action was the invasion of Afghanistan in October 2001. The Taliban regime, which had provided sanctuary to al-Qaeda, was swiftly overthrown, but the ensuing conflict evolved into a prolonged and complex war against insurgency and terrorism.

The Iraq War

In March 2003, the United States led a coalition to invade Iraq, based on the belief that Iraqi President

Saddam Hussein possessed weapons of mass destruction (WMDs) and posed a threat to international security. The invasion quickly toppled Hussein's regime, but no WMDs were found, and the initial military victory was followed by a protracted and violent insurgency. The Iraq War became highly controversial, with critics arguing that it was based on faulty intelligence and mismanaged in its execution.

Domestic Policies and Economic Challenges

Domestically, Bush's administration implemented several key policies, including significant tax cuts aimed at stimulating the economy. The Economic Growth and Tax Relief Reconciliation Act of 2001 and the Jobs and Growth Tax Relief Reconciliation Act of 2003 reduced income tax rates and were intended to boost economic growth.

Bush also focused on education reform, signing the No Child Left Behind Act in 2002, which aimed to improve educational standards and accountability in public schools. While the law had bipartisan support, it also faced criticism for its emphasis on standardized testing and its impact on schools.

In the latter part of Bush's presidency, the U.S. economy faced significant challenges, culminating in the financial crisis of 2007-2008. The collapse of major financial institutions, the bursting of the housing bubble, and the ensuing recession led to widespread economic hardship and required substantial government intervention, including the Emergency Economic Stabilization Act of 2008, which established the Troubled Asset Relief Program (TARP) to stabilise the financial system.

Hurricane Katrina

In 2005, Hurricane Katrina struck the Gulf Coast, causing catastrophic damage, particularly in New Orleans. The federal government's response to the disaster was widely criticized as slow and inadequate, exacerbating the humanitarian crisis. The handling of Hurricane Katrina highlighted issues of emergency preparedness and response, as well as systemic inequalities affecting vulnerable populations.

George W. Bush's presidency left a complex and contentious legacy. His leadership during the 9/11 attacks and the initial phases of the War on Terror garnered significant support, but the prolonged conflicts in Afghanistan and Iraq, along with the controversies surrounding the justification for the Iraq War, led to growing criticism and division.

Bush's domestic policies, including tax cuts and education reform, had mixed outcomes, and the financial crisis at the end of his presidency underscored the challenges facing the U.S. economy. Despite these difficulties, Bush's response to the 9/11 attacks and his efforts to combat terrorism have had a lasting impact on U.S. foreign and domestic policy.

Chapter - 18

OBAMA, THE FIRST AFRICAN AMERICAN PRESIDENT

Barack Obama's presidency marked a historic milestone in American history as he became the first African American President of the United States. Serving from 2009 to 2017, Obama's tenure was characterised by efforts to address the economic crisis, healthcare reform, and significant social and political change.

The 2008 Election and Inauguration

Barack Obama, a Democratic Senator from Illinois, won the 2008 presidential election against Republican Senator John McCain. His campaign, centred around the themes of "hope" and "change," resonated with a nation weary from economic hardship and political divisiveness. Obama's election was seen as a groundbreaking achievement, symbolising progress in the nation's ongoing struggle with racial equality.

The Great Recession and Economic Recovery

When Obama took office in January 2009, the United States was in the midst of the worst economic downturn since the Great Depression. The Great Recession had led to widespread job losses, a housing market collapse, and a severe financial crisis. In response, Obama and Congress passed the American Recovery and Reinvestment Act (ARRA) in February 2009, a $787 billion stimulus package aimed at spurring economic growth, saving jobs, and investing in infrastructure, education, and renewable energy.

The administration also implemented measures to stabilize the financial system, including the Troubled Asset Relief Program (TARP), initiated under President Bush, and the Dodd-Frank Wall Street Reform and Consumer Protection Act, which sought to increase financial regulation and prevent future crises.

Healthcare Reform: The Affordable Care Act

One of the most significant achievements of Obama's

presidency was the passage of the Affordable Care Act (ACA), also known as "Obamacare," in 2010. The ACA aimed to expand healthcare coverage, reduce costs, and improve the quality of care. Key provisions included the expansion of Medicaid, the establishment of health insurance exchanges, and the prohibition of denying coverage based on pre-existing conditions. The ACA faced fierce opposition from Republicans and numerous legal challenges, but it represented a landmark effort to reform the U.S. healthcare system.

Foreign Policy: Ending Wars and Shifting Focus

Obama's foreign policy sought to wind down the wars in Iraq and Afghanistan while addressing new global challenges. In 2011, U.S. forces captured and killed Osama bin Laden, the mastermind behind the 9/11 attacks, in a covert operation in Pakistan. The Iraq War officially ended in December 2011 with the withdrawal of U.S. troops, though the region remained unstable.

The Obama administration also emphasised diplomatic engagement and multilateralism. In 2015, the United States and five other world powers reached the Joint Comprehensive Plan of Action (JCPOA) with Iran, an agreement aimed at limiting Iran's nuclear program in exchange for lifting economic sanctions. Additionally, the administration pursued a "pivot to Asia," focusing on strengthening alliances and addressing rising challenges in the Asia-Pacific region.

Social Change and

Domestic Policy

Obama's presidency witnessed significant social change and progressive policies. In 2010, the administration repealed the "Don't Ask, Don't Tell" policy, allowing openly gay and lesbian individuals to serve in the military. The Supreme Court's decision in Obergefell v. Hodges in 2015 legalized same-sex marriage nationwide, reflecting changing societal attitudes toward LGBTQ+ rights.

The administration also focused on education reform, environmental protection, and criminal justice. The Race to the Top initiative incentivized states to pursue innovative education reforms, while the Clean Power Plan aimed to reduce carbon emissions from power plants. The Fair Sentencing Act of 2010 addressed disparities in sentencing for crack and powder cocaine offenses, and the administration took steps to reduce the federal prison population through clemency and sentencing reforms.

Challenges and Criticisms

Despite significant achievements, Obama's presidency faced numerous challenges and criticisms. The sluggish recovery from the Great Recession, persistent partisan gridlock in Congress, and the rise of the Tea Party movement created a polarized political environment. The administration's handling of the Syrian Civil War and the rise of ISIS drew criticism from various quarters, and the use of drone strikes in counterterrorism operations raised ethical and legal concerns.

The rollout of the ACA was marred by technical issues

with the HealthCare.gov website, and the law remained a contentious political issue, with ongoing debates over its effectiveness and impact. The administration also faced criticism for its immigration policies, including a record number of deportations and the failure to achieve comprehensive immigration reform.

Barack Obama's presidency left a lasting impact on the United States and the world. His election and tenure symbolized a significant step forward in the nation's journey toward racial equality and social progress. The ACA transformed the healthcare landscape, and his administration's efforts in education, environmental policy, and civil rights reflected a commitment to addressing complex societal challenges.

Obama's foreign policy emphasized diplomacy and multilateralism, though the Middle East remained a volatile and complex region. The economic recovery, while uneven, laid the groundwork for future growth and stability.

Part 6

THE TRUMP ERA AND BEYOND

- The Rise of Donald Trump
- The Trump Presidency: Policies and Controversies
- The 2020 Election and Beyond
- The Future of American Politics

Chapter - 19

THE RISE OF DONALD TRUMP

The rise of Donald Trump, the 45th President of the United States, represented a dramatic shift in American politics. His unexpected victory in the 2016 presidential election defied political norms and signalled a new era characterised by populism, polarisation, and an unorthodox approach to governance.

The 2016 Election

Donald Trump, a billionaire real estate mogul and reality television star, announced his candidacy for the presidency in June 2015. Running as a Republican, Trump's campaign was marked by its unconventional style, incendiary rhetoric, and focus on appealing to disaffected voters. His slogan, "Make America Great Again," resonated with many Americans who felt left behind by economic globalisation and disillusioned with the political establishment.

Trump's primary campaign was characterised by contentious debates and personal attacks, yet he emerged victorious against a crowded field of seasoned politicians. His outsider status, coupled with his promises to renegotiate trade deals, build a wall along the U.S.-Mexico border, and bring back manufacturing jobs, garnered him significant support among working-class voters.

Clinton vs. Trump: The General Election

The general election pitted Trump against Democratic nominee Hillary Clinton, a former Secretary of State, Senator, and First Lady. The campaign was one of the most divisive in modern American history, with both candidates facing substantial controversies. Clinton's use of a private email server during her tenure as Secretary of State and the FBI's subsequent investigation were focal points of Republican attacks.

Trump's campaign, meanwhile, was marred by numerous scandals, including allegations of sexual misconduct and the release of the Access Hollywood tape, in which he made lewd comments about women. Despite these controversies, Trump's message of change and his ability to tap into voter frustrations proved effective.

Election Night Shock

On November 8, 2016, Donald Trump won the presidency in a stunning upset. Despite losing the popular vote by nearly three million votes, he secured a decisive victory in the Electoral College, winning key battleground states like Pennsylvania, Michigan, and Wisconsin. Trump's victory was seen as a repudiation of the political establishment and a testament to the deep divisions within American society.

The Inauguration and Early Controversies

Donald Trump was inaugurated as the 45th President of the United States on January 20, 2017. His inaugural address emphasised themes of nationalism, economic protectionism, and a return of power to the American people. He vowed to end what he described as "American carnage" and to put "America First" in all policy decisions.

The early days of Trump's presidency were marked by a flurry of executive orders and contentious policy decisions. One of his first acts was to sign an executive order aimed at dismantling the Affordable Care Act, though efforts to repeal and replace the law ultimately failed in Congress. Trump's travel ban on several predominantly Muslim countries sparked widespread protests and legal challenges, setting the tone for a presidency characterised by frequent clashes with the judiciary and opposition groups.

The Russia Investigation

A major shadow over Trump's presidency was the investigation into Russian interference in the 2016 election. In May 2017, former FBI Director Robert Mueller was appointed as special counsel to investigate potential collusion between the Trump campaign and Russian officials. The investigation, which lasted nearly two years, led to numerous indictments and guilty pleas from Trump associates, though it did not establish a conspiracy between the campaign and Russia. However, the report did not exonerate Trump on allegations of obstruction of justice, leading to ongoing political controversy.

Immigration and Border Security

Immigration was a central focus of Trump's presidency. He implemented a zero-tolerance policy at the U.S.-Mexico border, leading to the separation of thousands of families and widespread condemnation. The construction of a border wall was a persistent promise, though funding and legal challenges limited its completion. Trump's administration also sought to end the Deferred Action for Childhood Arrivals (DACA) program, which provided protections for undocumented immigrants brought to the U.S. as children, though court rulings blocked the termination of the program.

Political Polarisation and Social Unrest

Trump's presidency exacerbated political polarisation and social unrest in the United States. His use of social media, particularly Twitter, to communicate directly with the public and attack opponents was unprecedented and often controversial. Trump's rhetoric and policies on issues such as race, immigration, and law enforcement sparked significant protests and movements, including the Women's March, Black Lives Matter protests, and demonstrations against police brutality.

The rise of Donald Trump reshaped American politics, bringing populism and nationalism to the forefront and challenging established norms and institutions. His presidency left a deeply divided nation, with fervent supporters and vehement critics. The 2020 election, in which Trump sought re-election against Democratic challenger Joe Biden, further underscored the polarised political landscape and the lasting impact of Trump's tenure on American society and governance.

Chapter - 20

THE TRUMP PRESIDENCY: POLICIES AND CONTROVERSIES

Donald Trump's presidency, spanning from 2017 to 2021, was characterised by a series of bold policies and numerous controversies that left a lasting impact on the United States and its position in the world. From economic reforms to immigration policies, Trump's administration pursued a distinctive agenda that often polarised public opinion and ignited widespread debate.

Economic Policies and Achievements

One of the hallmark achievements of Trump's presidency was the Tax Cuts and Jobs Act (TCJA) of 2017. This legislation significantly lowered the corporate tax rate from 35% to 21% and temporarily reduced individual tax rates. Proponents argued that these tax cuts spurred economic growth, increased corporate investments, and led to a boost in job creation. Critics, however, contended that the benefits disproportionately favored the wealthy and corporations while exacerbating the federal deficit.

Trump's administration also focused on deregulation, aiming to reduce what it perceived as burdensome regulations on businesses. Through executive orders and agency actions, the administration rolled back numerous regulations in areas such as environmental protection, labor, and consumer rights. While supporters claimed these efforts stimulated economic activity and innovation, opponents warned of potential long-term negative impacts on public health, safety, and the environment.

Trade and Tariff Policies

A key aspect of Trump's economic agenda was his approach to trade. Trump viewed existing trade agreements as unfavorable to American workers and industries and sought to renegotiate them. The United States-Mexico-Canada Agreement (USMCA), which replaced the North American Free Trade Agreement (NAFTA), aimed to create fairer trade terms for American farmers, workers, and businesses.

Trump also initiated a trade war with China, imposing tariffs on hundreds of billions of dollars' worth of Chinese goods. These tariffs were intended to address trade imbalances and intellectual property theft. The trade war had mixed results, with some sectors experiencing growth and others facing increased costs and market uncertainties. The long-term effects of these trade policies remain a topic of debate among economists and policymakers.

Immigration Policies and Border Security

Immigration was a central issue during Trump's presidency, and his administration implemented several controversial policies aimed at curbing illegal immigration and enhancing border security. The construction of a wall along the U.S.-Mexico border was a signature promise, though funding and legal challenges limited its progress. By the end of his term, approximately 450 miles of barriers had been built or reinforced.

The administration's zero-tolerance policy led to the separation of thousands of migrant families at the border, a practice that drew widespread condemnation both domestically and internationally. In response to the public outcry, Trump signed an executive order to end family separations, but the policy's legacy continued to impact immigration debates.

Trump also sought to end the Deferred Action for Childhood Arrivals (DACA) program, which protected undocumented immigrants brought to the U.S. as children from deportation. Legal challenges prevented the termination of DACA, and the program's fate remained uncertain. The administration implemented travel bans on several predominantly Muslim countries, citing national security concerns, a move that was met with significant legal challenges and protests.

Healthcare and Social Policies

Healthcare was another contentious area during Trump's presidency. The administration's efforts to repeal and replace the Affordable Care Act (ACA) faced significant obstacles. While the House of Representatives passed a repeal bill in 2017, the Senate ultimately rejected it, leaving the ACA largely intact. However, the administration succeeded in eliminating the individual mandate penalty, a key component of the ACA.

On social issues, Trump's presidency saw a rollback of various Obama-era regulations and protections. The administration's policies on transgender rights, including the ban on transgender individuals serving in the military, sparked significant debate and legal battles. The administration also expanded religious exemptions for employers regarding contraception coverage and rolled back protections for LGBTQ+ individuals in various areas.

Foreign Policy and International Relations

Trump's foreign policy was characterized by a departure from traditional alliances and a focus on an "America First" approach. He criticized NATO allies for not meeting their defense spending commitments and withdrew the U.S. from several international agreements, including the Paris Climate Accord and the Iran nuclear deal (Joint Comprehensive Plan of Action, JCPOA). Trump's administration also moved the U.S. embassy in Israel from Tel Aviv to Jerusalem, a decision that garnered both praise and criticism.

Relations with North Korea took an unprecedented turn as Trump engaged in direct diplomacy with North Korean leader Kim Jong-un. The two leaders held three high-profile summits, though tangible progress on denuclearization remained elusive.

Impeachments and Legal Challenges

Trump's presidency was marked by two impeachments, a historical first for a U.S. president. The first impeachment, in December 2019, centered on allegations that Trump abused his power by pressuring Ukraine to investigate political rival Joe Biden and his son, Hunter Biden. The House of Representatives approved two articles of impeachment: abuse of power and obstruction of Congress. The Senate acquitted Trump on both charges in February 2020.

In January 2021, following the storming of the U.S. Capitol by his supporters, Trump was impeached for a second time, charged with incitement of insurrection. The House passed the article of impeachment, but Trump was again acquitted by the Senate, with a majority voting to convict but failing to reach the necessary two-thirds threshold.

COVID-19 Pandemic Response

The COVID-19 pandemic, which emerged in late 2019 and spread globally in 2020, became a defining crisis of Trump's presidency. The administration's response was heavily criticized for its handling of the pandemic, including mixed messaging, delays in testing and contact tracing, and conflicts with state and local governments over lockdown measures and public health guidelines. Operation Warp Speed, a public-private partnership initiated by the administration, successfully accelerated the development and distribution of COVID-19 vaccines, which began rolling out in December 2020.

Donald Trump's presidency left a profound and polarizing impact on American politics and society. His unorthodox approach, characterized by direct communication through social media, reshaped the political landscape and galvanized both fervent support and intense opposition. The policies and controversies of his administration continue to influence debates on governance, democracy, and America's role in the world.

Chapter - 21

THE 2020 ELECTION AND BEYOND

The 2020 presidential election was one of the most consequential and contentious in American history. Amid a global pandemic, widespread social unrest, and a highly polarised political climate, the election resulted in the defeat of incumbent President Donald Trump and the election of former Vice President Joe Biden. The aftermath of the election saw unprecedented challenges to democratic norms and a nation grappling with profound divisions.

The Candidates and Campaigns

Joe Biden, a former Senator from Delaware and

Vice President under Barack Obama, emerged as the Democratic nominee after a competitive primary process. His running mate, Senator Kamala Harris, became the first woman of South Asian and African American descent to be nominated for national office by a major party. The Biden-Harris campaign focused on themes of unity, restoring the soul of America, and addressing the COVID-19 pandemic with a science-driven approach.

Donald Trump sought re-election, running on a platform of economic achievements, deregulation, and strong border policies. His campaign emphasized law and order, particularly in response to the protests and civil unrest following the killing of George Floyd by a police officer in Minneapolis. Trump's rallies and messaging continued to resonate with his core supporters, despite controversies and criticism of his administration's handling of the pandemic.

Impact of the COVID-19 Pandemic

The COVID-19 pandemic was a central issue in the 2020 election. The virus, which had infected millions and caused hundreds of thousands of deaths in the United States by election day, exposed deep divides in public health response and economic policy. The Trump administration's handling of the pandemic faced criticism for inconsistent messaging, delays in testing, and conflicts with health experts. Conversely, Trump touted Operation Warp Speed's success in accelerating vaccine development.

Biden's campaign prioritized a comprehensive and science-based approach to the pandemic, promising to implement a national strategy for testing, contact tracing, and vaccine distribution. The pandemic also influenced voting methods, with a significant increase in mail-in and early voting to reduce the risk of virus transmission at polling places.

Social Unrest and Racial Justice Movements

The summer of 2020 saw widespread protests and social unrest following the deaths of George Floyd, Breonna Taylor, and other Black Americans at the hands of law enforcement. The Black Lives Matter movement gained momentum, calling for police reform, racial justice, and an end to systemic racism. The national conversation on race and justice became a critical component of the election, with Trump positioning himself as a defender of law and order and Biden advocating for police reform and addressing racial inequalities.

Election Day and Results

The election took place on November 3, 2020, under the shadow of the pandemic and concerns about voter access and election integrity. Record numbers of Americans voted, with over 159 million ballots cast, making it the highest turnout in over a century. Due to the large volume of mail-in ballots, the results were not immediately known, leading to several days of counting in key battleground states.

On November 7, major news networks projected Joe Biden

as the winner of the election, having secured more than the necessary 270 electoral votes. Biden ultimately won 306 electoral votes to Trump's 232 and garnered over 81 million popular votes, the most in American history. Kamala Harris made history as the first female Vice President, as well as the first Black and South Asian Vice President.

Challenges to the Election Results

Following the election, President Trump and many of his supporters refused to accept the results, claiming widespread voter fraud without substantial evidence. The Trump campaign and its allies filed numerous lawsuits challenging the election outcomes in various states, but these efforts were largely unsuccessful. State and federal courts, including the Supreme Court, rejected most of the claims due to lack of evidence.

The refusal to concede and the perpetuation of unfounded claims of a stolen election contributed to heightened tensions and political polarization. These actions culminated in a significant and unprecedented event in American history.

The Capitol Insurrection

On January 6, 2021, as Congress convened to certify the Electoral College results, a violent mob of Trump supporters stormed the U.S. Capitol. The insurrection resulted in deaths, injuries, and widespread damage, marking a dark chapter in American democracy. The attack led to the evacuation of lawmakers and a temporary halt to the certification process, which resumed later that evening and confirmed Biden's victory.

The insurrection prompted a bipartisan condemnation and raised serious questions about the state of American democracy, the influence of misinformation, and the security of the nation's institutions. In the wake of the attack, Trump was impeached by the House of Representatives for a second time, charged with incitement of insurrection. He was acquitted by the Senate, with a majority voting to convict but failing to reach the required two-thirds threshold.

The Inauguration of Joe Biden

Joe Biden and Kamala Harris were inaugurated on January 20, 2021, under heavy security measures. Biden's inaugural address called for unity, healing, and a renewed commitment to democracy. His administration faced immediate challenges, including the ongoing pandemic, economic recovery, climate change, and restoring trust in government institutions.

The Future of American Politics

The 2020 election and its aftermath underscored the deep divisions within the United States. Moving forward, the Biden administration aimed to address these divides through a focus on bipartisan cooperation and addressing the nation's most pressing issues. The impact of Trump's presidency, the response to the Capitol insurrection, and ongoing debates over election integrity continue to shape the political landscape.

In summary, the 2020 election was a defining moment in American history, marked by unprecedented challenges and a transition of power in the face of deep national divisions. The election and its aftermath highlighted the resilience of American democracy, the importance of civic engagement, and the ongoing struggle to address the nation's most significant issues in an increasingly polarised environment.

Chapter - 22

THE FUTURE OF AMERICAN POLITICS

The political landscape of the United States has undergone significant changes, marked by increasing polarisation, shifting demographics, and evolving challenges. The future of American politics will be shaped by how leaders and citizens navigate these complexities and strive to uphold democratic principles.

Demographic Shifts and Electoral Implications

One of the most significant factors shaping the future of American politics is the nation's changing demographics. The United States is becoming more racially and ethnically diverse, with Hispanic, African American, Asian American, and other minority groups growing in numbers. This demographic shift is expected to influence voting patterns, policy priorities, and party dynamics.

Young voters, who are more diverse and generally more progressive, are becoming an increasingly influential demographic. Millennials and Generation Z have shown strong preferences for issues such as climate change, social justice, and economic equality. Their participation in elections will be crucial in shaping future political outcomes and policy directions.

Technological Advancements and Campaigning

The role of technology in politics has been transformative and will continue to evolve. Social media, digital advertising, and data analytics have become essential tools for political campaigns. These technologies allow for targeted messaging and voter engagement but also raise concerns about privacy, misinformation, and the influence of foreign entities.

Artificial intelligence and machine learning are poised to further revolutionize political campaigns and governance. These technologies can analyze vast amounts of data to predict voter behavior, optimize campaign strategies, and improve government services. However, they also present ethical challenges and the need for robust regulatory frameworks to prevent misuse and ensure transparency.

Economic Inequality and Policy Responses

Economic inequality remains a pressing issue in

American politics. The gap between the wealthy and the rest of the population has widened, exacerbating social and political tensions. Addressing economic inequality will require comprehensive policy responses, including tax reforms, increased access to education and healthcare, and policies that promote job creation and fair wages.

The future political landscape will likely see continued debates over the role of government in regulating the economy and providing social safety nets. Progressive movements advocating for wealth redistribution, universal basic income, and stronger labor rights are gaining momentum, influencing both Democratic and Republican platforms.

Climate Change and Environmental Policy

Climate change is an existential threat that demands urgent action. The future of American politics will be shaped by how effectively the nation addresses environmental challenges. Policies promoting renewable energy, carbon reduction, and sustainable practices will be at the forefront of political agendas.

Bipartisan support for addressing climate change has been growing, though significant differences remain on the specifics of policy approaches. The transition to a green economy presents both opportunities and challenges, including job creation in new industries and the potential economic impact on traditional energy sectors.

The Role of Social Movements

Social movements have played a pivotal role in shaping American politics and will continue to do so. Movements advocating for racial justice, gender equality, LGBTQ+ rights, and other social issues have mobilized millions and influenced public policy. These movements often operate outside traditional party structures, pushing for systemic change and holding leaders accountable.

The intersectionality of social movements, recognizing the interconnectedness of various forms of oppression and discrimination, will likely become more prominent. This holistic approach can lead to more comprehensive and inclusive policy solutions.

Challenges to Democracy and Governance

The events surrounding the 2020 election and the Capitol insurrection highlighted vulnerabilities in American democracy. Ensuring the integrity of elections, combating misinformation, and safeguarding democratic institutions will be critical tasks for future leaders.

Reforming the electoral system, including addressing gerrymandering, campaign finance, and voting rights, will be central to strengthening democracy. The rise of populism and authoritarianism poses additional challenges, requiring vigilance and a commitment to democratic norms and values.

Globalization and Foreign Policy

The United States' role on the global stage is evolving, with significant implications for domestic politics. Globalization has brought economic benefits but also challenges such as job displacement and cultural tensions. Balancing international cooperation with protecting domestic interests will be a key task for future administrations.

Foreign policy priorities will include managing relations with major powers such as China and Russia, addressing global health crises, and participating in international efforts to combat climate change. The approach to foreign policy will need to reflect a balance between traditional alliances and emerging global dynamics.

The Path Forward

The future of American politics is at a crossroads, with numerous challenges and opportunities ahead. Navigating this path will require visionary leadership, engaged citizenship, and a willingness to bridge divides. Embracing diversity, leveraging technology responsibly, and committing to social and economic justice can help build a more inclusive and resilient democracy.

Part - 7

THE MECHANICS OF AN ELECTION

- The Primary Process: Choosing Candidates
- Campaign Strategies and Tactics
- The Role of Media
- Election Night and Beyond

Chapter - 23

THE PRIMARY PROCESS: CHOOSING CANDIDATES

The primary process is a critical and complex component of the American electoral system. It is the mechanism through which political parties select their candidates for the general election. This chapter explores the primary process, its history, the different types of primaries, and the strategies candidates use to secure their party's nomination.

History and Evolution of Primaries

The primary process has evolved significantly since the early days of American politics. Initially, party candidates were selected by party leaders and delegates in conventions. This system often led to backroom deals and limited voter participation. The Progressive Era reforms of the early 20th century aimed to democratize the process, leading to the adoption of the primary system.

The first primary was held in Florida in 1901, but it was the 1912 election that saw the first significant use of primaries, with several states holding primary elections. Over time, the primary system expanded, becoming a standard practice for selecting party nominees.

Types of Primaries

Primaries come in several forms, each with its own rules and procedures. The main types include:

1. **Closed Primaries:** Only registered party members can vote in their respective party's primary. This system ensures that only dedicated party members influence the selection of candidates, but it can exclude independent or unaffiliated voters.
2. **Open Primaries:** Any registered voter can participate in either party's primary, regardless of party affiliation. This system allows for broader participation but can lead to strategic voting by members of the opposing party.
3. **Semi-Closed Primaries:** Registered party members and unaffiliated voters can participate, but voters registered with another party cannot. This strikes a balance between closed and open primaries, allowing some flexibility while maintaining party

control.
4. **Blanket Primaries:** All candidates, regardless of party affiliation, are listed on the same ballot. Voters can choose candidates from different parties for different offices. This system is rare and was mostly replaced by the "top-two" primary system in states like California and Washington.
5. **Caucuses:** Unlike primaries, caucuses are meetings of party members who discuss and vote for their preferred candidates. Caucuses involve more active participation and deliberation but can be less accessible to voters than primaries.

The Primary Calendar

The timing of primaries and caucuses is crucial and can significantly influence the outcome of the nomination process. The primary season traditionally begins with the Iowa caucuses and the New Hampshire primary. These early contests are critical because they can shape perceptions of candidate viability and momentum.

Super Tuesday, a key date in the primary calendar, involves multiple states holding primaries on the same day. Success on Super Tuesday can propel a candidate to front-runner status. However, the primary calendar can be a point of contention, with debates over the influence of early states and calls for a more equitable system.

Delegate Allocation and Conventions

Candidates compete to win delegates, who will support them at their party's national convention. Delegate allocation rules vary by party and state. Democrats use a proportional allocation system, where delegates are distributed based on the percentage of the vote each candidate receives. Republicans use a mix of proportional, winner-take-all, and hybrid systems.

The national conventions, held in the summer before the general election, are where the official nomination occurs. Delegates cast their votes, and the candidate with the majority of delegates becomes the party's nominee. Conventions also serve as a platform for party unity, policy discussions, and launching the general election campaign.

Strategies for Winning Primaries

Candidates must develop strategies to navigate the complex primary process. Key strategies include:

1. **Building a Strong Ground Game:** Organizing volunteers, canvassing, and mobilising voters are essential for success, especially in states with caucuses.
2. **Fundraising and Media:** Raising funds to finance campaign activities and advertising is crucial. Media coverage, both traditional and social, plays a significant role in shaping voter perceptions.
3. **Policy Positioning:** Candidates must balance appealing to their party's base with maintaining electability in the general election. This often involves taking clear stances on key issues while avoiding extreme positions that could alienate general election voters.
4. **Debates and Public Appearances:** Performing well in debates and public appearances can boost a

candidate's visibility and credibility. Engaging with voters through town halls and events is also important for building support.
5. **Adapting to the Primary Calendar:** Candidates must strategically allocate resources and time to key states, particularly those early in the primary calendar. Success in early states can generate momentum and media attention.

Challenges of the Primary System

The primary system faces several criticisms and challenges:

1. **Voter Turnout:** Primary elections often have lower voter turnout compared to general elections, which can skew results towards more active and engaged party members.
2. **Influence of Early States:** The disproportionate influence of early states like Iowa and New Hampshire can shape the race before a majority of voters have a chance to participate.
3. **Complex Rules:** The varying rules and procedures across states can confuse voters and complicate the process for candidates.
4. **Polarisation:** The primary system can incentivize candidates to appeal to the party base, potentially leading to more polarised candidates in the general election.

Despite these challenges, the primary process remains a foundational element of American democracy, allowing voters to have a direct impact on the selection of their party's candidates.

Chapter - 24

CAMPAIGN STRATEGIES AND TACTICS

Campaign strategies and tactics are pivotal in determining the outcome of elections. From grassroots organising to high-tech data analytics, modern campaigns employ a variety of methods to reach and persuade voters. This chapter explores the key components of campaign strategies, the evolution of tactics, and the impact of technology and media on the electoral process.

The Art of Campaign Strategy

Campaign strategy involves a comprehensive plan to win an election. It encompasses message development, target audience identification, resource allocation, and overall coordination. Successful strategies are built on a deep understanding of the electorate and the political landscape.

1. **Message Development:** Crafting a compelling message is central to any campaign. The message must resonate with voters and address their concerns. Effective messages often focus on key issues, personal narratives, and a clear vision for the future. The message should be consistent across all campaign platforms and tailored to different voter segments.
2. **Target Audience:** Identifying and understanding target voter demographics is crucial. Campaigns use data to segment the electorate into various groups based on factors like age, gender, income, education, and geographic location. By understanding these segments, campaigns can tailor their messages and outreach efforts to address specific concerns and preferences.
3. **Resource Allocation:** Campaigns must manage their resources efficiently, including time, money, and personnel. This involves budgeting for advertising, staff salaries, events, and other expenses. Campaigns must also decide how to allocate resources geographically, focusing efforts on battleground states or districts where the election is expected to be close.
4. **Coordination and Organization:** A well-organized campaign is essential for executing strategy effectively. This includes managing staff, volunteers, and campaign offices. Clear communication and coordination are necessary to ensure that all aspects of the campaign work together towards common goals.

Tactics and Tools

Campaign tactics are the specific actions and methods used to implement strategy. These tactics can vary widely but generally fall into several key areas:

1. **Advertising:** Political advertising is a major component of campaign tactics. This includes television, radio, digital ads, and print media. Advertisements are designed to raise candidate visibility, convey key messages, and influence voter perceptions. The choice of media and messaging strategy often depends on the target audience and campaign budget.
2. **Grassroots Organising:** Grassroots organising involves mobilising local supporters to engage in activities such as canvassing, phone banking, and organising events. Grassroots efforts help build a base of enthusiastic supporters who can influence their communities and drive voter turnout.
3. **Debates and Public Appearances:** Candidates participate in debates and public events to showcase their policies, respond to opponents, and connect with voters. Performance in debates can significantly impact public perception and campaign momentum.
4. **Digital and Social Media:** The rise of digital and social media has transformed campaign tactics. Campaigns use social media platforms to engage with voters, share information, and drive conversation. Digital tools also enable targeted advertising and voter outreach, leveraging data to optimise messaging and engagement.

5. **Direct Mail and Email:** Direct mail and email campaigns are used to reach voters with personalized messages. These tactics allow campaigns to provide detailed information, solicit donations, and encourage voter participation.
6. **Get-Out-The-Vote (GOTV) Efforts:** GOTV efforts are crucial in the final days of a campaign. These tactics aim to ensure that supporters actually cast their ballots. This includes reminders, transportation assistance, and providing information about polling locations and procedures.

The Role of Polling and Data Analytics

Polling and data analytics play a significant role in modern campaigns. Campaigns use polls to gauge public opinion, track changes in voter preferences, and refine their strategies. Data analytics allows campaigns to identify trends, measure the effectiveness of tactics, and make data-driven decisions.

1. **Polling:** Polling provides insights into voter attitudes and preferences. It helps campaigns understand which issues resonate with voters, how candidates are perceived, and which segments of the electorate are most supportive. Polls can also inform strategic decisions, such as which issues to emphasize and where to focus resources.
2. **Data Analytics:** Advanced data analytics tools allow campaigns to analyze voter data and optimize their strategies. This includes using voter files, social media data, and consumer behavior data to create detailed voter profiles and target communications

more effectively.

Challenges and Controversies

Campaign strategies and tactics are not without challenges and controversies:

1. **Negative Advertising:** Negative ads, which attack opponents rather than promote the candidate, can be effective but are often criticized for contributing to a toxic political climate. They can also backfire if voters perceive them as unfair or misleading.
2. **Misinformation and Disinformation:** The spread of misinformation and disinformation, particularly on social media, poses a significant challenge. Campaigns must navigate the potential for false information to influence voter perceptions and behavior.
3. **Election Integrity:** Ensuring the integrity of the election process is a critical concern. Campaigns must address issues related to voter suppression, election security, and the accurate counting of votes.
4. **Ethical Considerations:** Campaign tactics must be balanced with ethical considerations. This includes avoiding deceptive practices, respecting voter privacy, and maintaining transparency in campaign financing.

The Future of Campaigning

The future of campaign strategies and tactics will likely be shaped by ongoing technological advancements and changing voter behaviours. Innovations in digital tools, data analytics, and communication methods will continue to transform how campaigns operate.

Campaigns will need to adapt to evolving trends, including the increasing importance of social media, the growing influence of younger voters, and the need for transparency and accountability. The ability to effectively engage with voters, address their concerns, and navigate the complexities of modern campaigning will be essential for success in future elections.

Chapter - 25

THE ROLE OF MEDIA

The media plays a crucial role in shaping the electoral landscape and influencing voter behaviour. From traditional newspapers and broadcast television to digital platforms and social media, media outlets are integral in providing information, framing issues, and shaping public perception. This chapter examines the role of media in elections, the impact of media coverage, and the evolving nature of media influence in modern campaigns.

The Traditional Media Landscape

Historically, traditional media—newspapers, radio, and television—served as the primary sources of news and information during elections.

1. **Newspapers:** Newspapers have long been a key source of political reporting and commentary. Editorial endorsements, investigative journalism, and news coverage have influenced public opinion and candidate visibility. While the influence of print media has waned with the rise of digital platforms, major newspapers still play a significant role in shaping political discourse.
2. **Radio:** Radio provided a new platform for political communication in the early 20th century. Radio broadcasts allowed candidates to reach a wide audience with speeches and advertisements. Talk radio, particularly, has become a powerful medium for political commentary and mobilization, often reflecting and amplifying particular ideological viewpoints.
3. **Television:** Television revolutionized political campaigns by providing a visual platform for candidates to present themselves and their messages. Campaign ads, news coverage, and televised debates have become central elements of modern elections. The advent of cable television further fragmented the media landscape, creating a multitude of channels and increasing the variety of political programming.

The Rise of Digital Media

The rise of digital media has transformed the political landscape, providing new opportunities and challenges for campaigns, voters, and media organisations.

1. **Online News:** The internet has become a

major source of news and information. Online news platforms, including digital versions of traditional media and new digital-only outlets, provide real-time updates and in-depth analysis. However, the proliferation of news sources also raises concerns about information quality and the spread of misinformation.

2. **Social Media:** Social media platforms like Facebook, Twitter, Instagram, and TikTok have become central to political communication. Candidates and campaigns use social media to engage with voters, share messages, and respond to current events. Social media also enables real-time interaction and feedback, allowing campaigns to tailor their messages and strategies quickly.

3. **Political Advertising:** Digital platforms offer sophisticated tools for targeted political advertising. Campaigns can use data analytics to target specific voter segments with customised messages, increasing the effectiveness of their outreach. However, this also raises concerns about privacy, data security, and the potential for manipulation.

Media Influence and Voter Perception

Media coverage has a profound impact on how voters perceive candidates and issues.

1. **Framing and Agenda-Setting:** Media outlets play a key role in framing political issues and setting the agenda. The way stories are presented—highlighting certain aspects while downplaying others—can

influence public perception and prioritize particular issues in the political discourse.
2. **Coverage Bias:** Media bias can affect how candidates and issues are portrayed. Different media outlets may emphasize different aspects of a campaign or provide favourable or unfavourable coverage based on their editorial stance. This can shape voter opinions and contribute to polarised perceptions.
3. **Candidate Image:** Media coverage often focuses on candidates' images and personal characteristics. The portrayal of candidates in the media can impact their public image and influence voter trust and likability. Candidates' appearances, mannerisms, and responses to media questions are scrutinised and can affect their campaign's success.

The Impact of Media on Campaign Strategies

Campaigns have adapted their strategies to leverage the media's influence effectively.

1. **Media Training:** Candidates undergo media training to improve their performance in interviews, debates, and public appearances. Effective communication with the media is crucial for shaping positive coverage and managing potential controversies.
2. **News Management:** Campaigns employ news management strategies to control the narrative and

maximize positive coverage. This includes issuing press releases, organizing press conferences, and responding promptly to news events.
3. **Crisis Communication:** Managing crises and negative stories is a key aspect of campaign strategy. Campaigns develop crisis communication plans to address issues that arise and mitigate damage to the candidate's reputation.

The Future of Media and Elections

The future of media in elections will be shaped by ongoing technological advancements and changes in voter behaviour.

1. **Emerging Technologies:** Innovations such as artificial intelligence, virtual reality, and augmented reality may create new opportunities for political communication and engagement. These technologies could enhance voter experiences but also introduce new challenges related to information accuracy and privacy.
2. **Changing Media Consumption Habits:** As media consumption habits continue to evolve, campaigns will need to adapt their strategies to reach voters through emerging platforms and formats. This may involve developing new forms of digital content and engaging with voters through interactive and immersive experiences.
3. **Regulation and Ethics:** The role of media in elections may prompt discussions about regulation and ethical standards. Balancing freedom of the press with the need to address misinformation

and ensure fair coverage will be important for maintaining the integrity of the electoral process.

Chapter - 26

ELECTION NIGHT AND BEYOND

Election Night is the climax of a long and arduous campaign, a time when voters, candidates, and the media await the final results that will determine the outcome of the election. However, the significance of Election Night extends beyond just the tallying of votes. This chapter explores the events and processes of Election Night, the role of media and technology, the aftermath of the election, and the transition to a new administration.

The Build-Up to Election Night

As Election Day approaches, the intensity of campaign activities typically reaches a peak. Candidates make their final appeals to voters, participate in last-minute events, and prepare for the transition to the next phase of their campaigns.

1. **Final Campaign Push:** In the days leading

up to Election Day, candidates focus on mobilising supporters and getting out the vote (GOTV). This final push often involves rallies, canvassing, and targeted outreach efforts to ensure that their supporters cast their ballots.
2. **Polling Stations and Voting:** On Election Day, polling stations open across the country, and voters head to the polls to cast their votes. Election officials and poll workers are responsible for ensuring a smooth voting process, addressing any issues that arise, and maintaining the integrity of the election.

Election Night Coverage and Results

Election Night coverage is a major event in itself, involving extensive media coverage, live updates, and real-time analysis.

1. **Media Coverage:** News networks and media outlets provide continuous coverage of Election Night, reporting on results as they come in, analyzing trends, and providing updates from key battleground states. Anchors, analysts, and reporters offer insights into the implications of the results and the status of the race.
2. **Vote Counting and Reporting:** Vote counting begins as polls close, with results reported from various precincts and districts. The process involves tabulating votes, verifying results, and ensuring accuracy. Media organisations use exit polls, partial results, and statistical models to project outcomes and call races.
3. **Projection and Results:** Based on the results

and projections, media outlets announce winners in various races. These projections are made with careful consideration of the data, but they are not official until all votes are counted and certified. Candidates and their campaigns closely monitor the results and prepare for potential scenarios.

Post-Election Procedures

Once the initial results are in, the focus shifts to the post-election process, including the certification of results, potential legal challenges, and the transition to a new administration.

1. **Certification of Results:** The certification process involves verifying and officially confirming the vote totals. This process varies by state but generally includes reviewing and reconciling results from different precincts, addressing any discrepancies, and ensuring compliance with election laws.
2. **Concession and Acceptance Speeches:** Following the results, losing candidates typically deliver concession speeches, acknowledging their defeat and offering congratulations to the winner. Winning candidates deliver acceptance speeches, outlining their vision for the future and thanking supporters. These speeches are significant moments that set the tone for the transition and the upcoming administration.
3. **Legal Challenges and Recounts:** In some cases, candidates may challenge the results or request recounts if the margin of victory is very narrow or if there are concerns about the accuracy of the count. Legal challenges and recounts can delay the final

certification of results and impact the transition process.

The Transition to the New Administration

The transition period is a critical phase following the election, involving the preparation and handover of responsibilities from the outgoing administration to the incoming one.

1. **Transition Planning:** The incoming administration begins planning for governance, including selecting cabinet members, setting policy priorities, and preparing for the challenges of taking office. Transition teams work to ensure a smooth handover and address any immediate issues.
2. **Inauguration:** The inauguration marks the formal beginning of a new administration. The president-elect is sworn in, delivering an inaugural address that outlines their vision and agenda for the country. The inauguration is a significant ceremonial event that symbolizes the peaceful transfer of power.
3. **Policy Implementation:** After taking office, the new administration begins implementing its policy agenda. This involves setting up new initiatives, issuing executive orders, and working with Congress to advance legislative priorities. The transition period also includes addressing any pressing issues and establishing relationships with key stakeholders.

Public Reaction and

Media Analysis

The aftermath of the election involves public reaction and media analysis, which can shape perceptions and influence the early days of the new administration.

1. **Public Reaction:** Voters, supporters, and critics react to the election results and the transition process. Public opinion can be influenced by the new administration's early actions, the handling of any controversies, and the effectiveness of the transition.
2. **Media Analysis:** Media outlets analyse the results and the implications for the political landscape. This includes evaluating the performance of candidates, the impact of campaign strategies, and the significance of the election outcomes for future political dynamics.

Looking Ahead

As the new administration settles in, the focus shifts to the implementation of policies, addressing key issues, and preparing for future elections. The lessons learned from Election Night and the transition process can provide valuable insights for future campaigns and electoral cycles.

Conclusion

THE ENDURING ALLURE OF THE PRESIDENCY

- The Impact of Presidents
- Challenges and Opportunities for Future Leaders
- Engaging in the Political Process

Chapter - 27

THE IMPACT OF PRESIDENTS

The presidency of the United States is more than just a position of power; it is a symbol of the nation's ideals, a reflection of its values, and a central figure in shaping its history. This chapter explores the enduring legacy and impact of American presidents, examining how they have influenced the country's trajectory and the ways in which their presidencies continue to resonate with and inspire future generations.

Shaping National Identity

Presidents play a crucial role in shaping the national identity and guiding the country through periods of change and challenge.

1. **Defining Moments:** Many presidencies are defined by critical moments in American history. From George Washington's leadership in establishing the new nation to Franklin D. Roosevelt's New Deal

during the Great Depression, and from John F. Kennedy's vision of a "New Frontier" to Barack Obama's historic election as the first African American president, these defining moments have left a lasting imprint on the nation's identity.
2. **Crisis Management:** Presidents are often judged by their ability to manage crises and navigate through turbulent times. Their responses to events such as wars, economic downturns, and social upheavals can significantly impact their legacy and the course of the country's history. The way presidents handle these challenges reflects their leadership qualities and their ability to inspire confidence and hope in the American people.
3. **Symbolism and Representation:** The presidency is also a symbol of the nation's values and aspirations. Presidents often represent the collective hopes and dreams of the American people, and their actions and words can embody the nation's ideals of democracy, freedom, and justice. This symbolic role adds to the allure of the presidency, making it a powerful and enduring figure in American life.

The Evolution of Presidential Leadership

Over time, the nature of presidential leadership has evolved, influenced by changes in society, technology, and the political landscape.

1. **Changing Expectations:** The expectations of

the presidency have shifted throughout history. Early presidents were seen as figures of moral authority and leadership, while modern presidents are expected to be active leaders in policy-making, international relations, and crisis management. The evolving role of the presidency reflects broader changes in the nation's expectations and needs.
2. **Communication and Media:** The way presidents communicate with the public has transformed with advancements in media technology. From radio addresses and television broadcasts to social media and digital platforms, presidents have adapted their communication strategies to connect with voters and shape public opinion. This evolution in communication has expanded the reach and influence of the presidency.
3. **Policy Innovations:** Each presidency brings its own set of policy innovations and reforms. Presidents have introduced landmark legislation, executive orders, and programs that address the pressing issues of their time. These innovations have shaped the course of American history and continue to influence policy debates and governance.

The Enduring Influence of Presidential Legacies

The legacies of presidents extend beyond their time in office, influencing future generations and the direction of the country.

1. **Historical Impact:** The impact of a presidency is often evaluated in historical context. Presidential legacies are studied and analysed by

historians, scholars, and the public, contributing to the ongoing discourse about their contributions and achievements. The enduring influence of presidential legacies can shape national values and priorities.

2. **Inspiration and Role Models:** Presidents often serve as role models and sources of inspiration for future leaders and citizens. Their leadership qualities, vision, and accomplishments can motivate individuals to engage in public service, advocate for change, and contribute to the nation's progress. The stories of presidents who have overcome adversity or made significant contributions continue to inspire and resonate with people.

3. **Institutional Influence:** The presidency itself is an enduring institution that continues to shape the functioning of American government and politics. The precedents set by past presidents, the evolution of executive powers, and the role of the presidency in the balance of power all contribute to the ongoing influence of the office.

The Future of the Presidency

As the nation looks to the future, the presidency will continue to play a central role in shaping American life and addressing new challenges.

1. **Adapting to Change:** Future presidents will face new and evolving challenges, including technological advancements, global issues, and shifts in societal values. The ability to adapt to these changes while upholding the principles of democracy and leadership will be crucial for future

presidents.
2. **Maintaining Relevance:** The presidency must continue to maintain its relevance and connection with the American people. This involves addressing contemporary issues, engaging with diverse communities, and fostering a sense of unity and purpose.
3. **Preserving the Legacy:** The preservation of the presidency's legacy involves a commitment to the core values of the office and the principles of democratic governance. Future presidents will build on the legacies of their predecessors while shaping their own contributions to the nation's history.

Chapter - 28

CHALLENGES AND OPPORTUNITIES FOR FUTURE LEADERS

As the landscape of American politics evolves, future presidents will face a unique set of challenges and opportunities that will shape their leadership and impact. This chapter delves into the key issues that future leaders will need to address, the opportunities available for advancing the nation, and the strategies that can help navigate the complex political terrain of the 21st century.

Emerging Challenges for Future Presidents

1. **Political Polarization:** The increasing divide

between political parties and ideologies presents a significant challenge for future presidents. Navigating this polarization requires a delicate balance between addressing partisan concerns and finding common ground. Effective leadership will involve bridging divides, fostering bipartisanship, and working towards solutions that benefit the entire nation.

2. **Economic Inequality:** Economic inequality remains a pressing issue, with growing disparities in wealth and income affecting social stability and economic mobility. Future presidents will need to address these disparities through policies that promote equitable growth, access to education, healthcare, and opportunities for all citizens.
3. **Climate Change and Environmental Sustainability:** Climate change presents an urgent and global challenge that demands immediate action. Future presidents will need to prioritize environmental sustainability, implement policies to combat climate change, and promote international cooperation on environmental issues.
4. **Technological Disruption:** Rapid advancements in technology, including artificial intelligence, automation, and digital transformation, pose both opportunities and challenges. Future leaders will need to manage the impact of these technologies on the workforce, privacy, and cybersecurity while harnessing their potential for innovation and progress.
5. **Global Geopolitical Shifts:** The international landscape is constantly evolving, with shifts in power dynamics, emerging global threats, and

complex diplomatic relationships. Future presidents will need to navigate these geopolitical changes, strengthen alliances, and address global challenges such as conflicts, terrorism, and human rights issues.

6. **Public Trust and Transparency:** Restoring and maintaining public trust in government institutions is a crucial challenge. Future presidents will need to prioritize transparency, ethical governance, and accountability to rebuild confidence in the political system and ensure that government actions align with public interests.

Opportunities for Advancing the Nation

1. **Innovation and Technology:** Embracing innovation and technology offers significant opportunities for advancing the nation. Future presidents can leverage technological advancements to drive economic growth, improve public services, and address societal challenges. Investing in research and development, promoting STEM education, and supporting technological entrepreneurship will be key to harnessing these opportunities.

2. **Social Progress and Equity:** Advancing social progress and promoting equity are critical opportunities for future leaders. This includes addressing systemic injustices, promoting diversity and inclusion, and ensuring equal rights and opportunities for all individuals. Future presidents can champion policies that advance civil rights,

gender equality, and social justice.
3. **Healthcare and Public Health:** Improving healthcare systems and public health outcomes presents a significant opportunity for future presidents. This involves expanding access to quality healthcare, addressing public health crises, and implementing policies that promote wellness and disease prevention.
4. **Economic Renewal and Infrastructure:** Investing in economic renewal and infrastructure development can drive long-term growth and prosperity. Future leaders have the opportunity to revitalize aging infrastructure, promote sustainable development, and create economic opportunities through strategic investments in transportation, energy, and technology.
5. **Educational Reform:** Education is a key driver of economic and social progress. Future presidents can champion educational reform that enhances access to quality education, addresses disparities, and prepares the workforce for the demands of a rapidly changing economy.
6. *Strengthening Democracy:* Enhancing democratic institutions and processes is an ongoing opportunity for future leaders. This includes promoting electoral integrity, reforming campaign finance, and encouraging civic engagement to ensure a vibrant and participatory democracy.

Strategies for Effective Leadership

1. **Building Coalitions:** Effective leadership

often requires building coalitions and fostering collaboration across party lines. Future presidents can work to cultivate relationships with legislators, stakeholders, and community leaders to achieve common goals and address pressing issues.

2. **Communicating with Transparency:** Clear and transparent communication is essential for gaining public trust and support. Future presidents should prioritize honest and open dialogue with the American people, provide regular updates on policies and initiatives, and address concerns and challenges proactively.

3. **Prioritizing Policy Over Politics:** Focusing on policy solutions rather than political considerations can help future presidents address the nation's most pressing issues effectively. By prioritizing the needs of the country and seeking evidence-based solutions, leaders can build credibility and achieve meaningful results.

4. **Fostering Inclusivity and Engagement:** Engaging diverse communities and fostering inclusivity in governance can enhance the effectiveness and legitimacy of leadership. Future presidents should seek input from a broad range of voices, promote diversity in appointments, and ensure that policies reflect the interests of all Americans.

5. **Adapting to Change:** The ability to adapt to changing circumstances and emerging challenges is crucial for effective leadership. Future presidents should be flexible and open to new ideas, willing to reassess strategies, and responsive to the evolving needs of the nation.

6. **Cultivating Resilience:** Leading a nation requires

resilience in the face of adversity. Future presidents must be prepared to navigate setbacks, handle crises, and maintain focus on long-term goals. Cultivating resilience and perseverance will be essential for overcoming challenges and achieving success.

Chapter - 29

ENGAGING IN THE POLITICAL PROCESS

The presidency, with its profound influence and symbolic significance, underscores the importance of engaging in the political process. This chapter explores how citizens, leaders, and institutions can actively participate in and shape the political landscape, ensuring that democracy remains vibrant and effective.

The Role of Citizens in Democracy

Active citizen engagement is fundamental to a healthy democracy. Citizens have a variety of ways to participate in the political process, each contributing to the functioning and integrity of the democratic system.

1. **Voting:** Voting is one of the most direct and impactful ways citizens can influence government and policy. Participating in elections, whether local, state, or national, enables individuals to choose representatives and shape the direction of government. Voter education and outreach are crucial in ensuring that all eligible citizens are informed and motivated to cast their ballots.
2. **Advocacy and Activism:** Advocacy and activism allow citizens to express their views, support causes, and drive change. By engaging in advocacy—whether through lobbying, campaigning, or organizing community events—individuals and groups can influence policy decisions and raise awareness about important issues. Activism can also involve participating in protests, petitions, and grassroots movements.
3. **Public Discourse and Debate:** Engaging in public discourse and debate is essential for a functioning democracy. Citizens can contribute to discussions on political issues, policy proposals, and societal challenges through various platforms, including town hall meetings, online forums, and public hearings. Constructive debate helps to refine ideas, build consensus, and foster democratic deliberation.
4. **Community Involvement:** Community involvement, such as volunteering for local organizations or participating in civic groups, strengthens democratic engagement at the grassroots level. By addressing local needs and working collaboratively with others, citizens contribute to the overall well-being of their communities and support democratic values.

The Importance of Leadership and Accountability

Effective leadership is crucial for the health and effectiveness of democratic institutions. Leaders, including elected officials, public servants, and community leaders, play a key role in shaping policy, guiding governance, and ensuring accountability.

1. **Ethical Leadership:** Ethical leadership involves acting with integrity, transparency, and responsibility. Leaders are expected to uphold democratic principles, make decisions based on the public good, and avoid conflicts of interest. Maintaining high ethical standards helps build public trust and ensures that governance is conducted with fairness and respect.
2. **Transparency and Accountability:** Transparency and accountability are vital for ensuring that leaders are answerable to the public. Open communication about decision-making processes, financial disclosures, and policy outcomes fosters trust and allows citizens to hold leaders accountable. Mechanisms such as oversight committees, audits, and investigative journalism contribute to maintaining accountability.
3. **Effective Governance:** Effective governance requires leaders to address complex issues, implement sound policies, and respond to the needs of the population. Leaders must balance competing interests, manage resources efficiently, and collaborate with other stakeholders to achieve positive outcomes. Continuous evaluation and

improvement of governance practices help to enhance effectiveness and address challenges.

The Role of Institutions in Democracy

Institutions, including government bodies, political parties, and non-governmental organizations (NGOs), play a crucial role in maintaining democratic processes and ensuring effective governance.

1. **Government Institutions:** Government institutions, such as the executive, legislative, and judicial branches, are foundational to the functioning of democracy. These institutions are responsible for creating, implementing, and interpreting laws and policies. Ensuring their independence, competence, and responsiveness is essential for upholding democratic principles and protecting citizens' rights.
2. **Political Parties:** Political parties serve as vehicles for organizing political activity, representing diverse viewpoints, and facilitating electoral competition. Parties play a role in shaping policy platforms, recruiting candidates, and mobilizing voters. Healthy party systems contribute to a dynamic and representative political landscape.
3. **Non-Governmental Organizations (NGOs):** NGOs and civil society organizations contribute to democratic engagement by advocating for specific causes, providing services, and holding governments accountable. NGOs play a role in promoting social justice, environmental sustainability, and human rights, and their efforts complement governmental

and political activities.

Civic Education and Engagement

Civic education and engagement are essential for preparing citizens to participate effectively in the political process and contribute to a healthy democracy.

1. **Civic Education:** Civic education programs help individuals understand the principles of democracy, the functions of government, and their roles as citizens. Educational initiatives at schools, universities, and community organizations promote awareness of civic responsibilities and encourage informed participation.
2. **Youth Engagement:** Engaging young people in the political process is crucial for sustaining democratic involvement. Programs that involve youth in decision-making, offer internships, and provide opportunities for leadership development help to cultivate the next generation of informed and active citizens.
3. **Public Engagement Campaigns:** Public engagement campaigns, including voter registration drives, informational workshops, and community outreach, help to increase awareness and participation in the political process. These campaigns aim to reach diverse populations and encourage broad-based involvement.

Looking Ahead

As the political landscape continues to evolve, ongoing engagement and participation will be crucial for maintaining a vibrant democracy. Citizens, leaders, and institutions must adapt to changing circumstances, address emerging challenges, and continue to uphold democratic values.

1. **Embracing New Technologies:** The integration of new technologies, such as digital platforms and social media, presents both opportunities and challenges for political engagement. Future efforts should focus on leveraging these technologies to enhance democratic participation while addressing issues related to misinformation and privacy.
2. **Promoting Inclusivity:** Ensuring that all voices are heard and valued is essential for a robust democracy. Efforts to promote inclusivity and address systemic barriers to participation will strengthen democratic processes and contribute to a more equitable society.
3. **Sustaining Democratic Values:** The enduring allure of the presidency and the broader political system is rooted in democratic values such as freedom, equality, and justice. Upholding these values and continuously working to improve the democratic process will ensure that the principles of democracy remain vibrant and effective.

BONUS CHAPTERS

- Vice Presidents: The Unsung Heroes
- First Ladies: Influence from the White House
- Campaign Finance and Lobbying
- The Electoral Map: Swing States and Battlegrounds
- Third-Party Candidates: The Outsiders
- Voter Turnout and Demographics

Chapter - 1

VICE PRESIDENTS: THE UNSUNG HEROES

Vice Presidents of the United States often play a crucial yet understated role in the governance and political landscape of the country. Though frequently overshadowed by the President, Vice Presidents have been integral to the functioning of the executive branch, offering significant contributions and influence in various ways. This chapter explores the evolution, duties, and impact of Vice Presidents, highlighting their key roles and providing detailed insights into their contributions to American political history.

The Evolution of the Vice Presidency

The role of the Vice President has evolved significantly since its inception, adapting to the changing political and administrative needs of the country.

1. **Early Days and Constitutional Foundations:** The office of Vice President was established by the U.S. Constitution in 1787. Initially, the Vice President's primary duty was to preside over the Senate and cast tie-breaking votes. The role was largely ceremonial with minimal influence on policy-making or executive decisions. The first Vice President, John Adams, famously remarked that the office was "the most insignificant office that ever the invention of man contrived or his imagination conceived."
2. **Expansion of Responsibilities:** Over time, the role of the Vice President expanded beyond its original scope. During the 19th and early 20th centuries, Vice Presidents were often seen as placeholders or political allies chosen for balancing tickets. However, as the complexities of modern governance grew, so did the responsibilities of the Vice Presidency. The position began to include more substantive duties such as participating in policy discussions, representing the administration domestically and internationally, and stepping in during presidential incapacitation.
3. **Modern Era and Increased Influence:** In recent decades, Vice Presidents have played a more prominent and active role in the administration. The Vice Presidency has become a platform for influential political figures, often tasked with leading major initiatives, managing key policy areas, and serving as a key advisor to the President. Notable

Vice Presidents like Lyndon B. Johnson, Richard Nixon, Al Gore, and Joe Biden have significantly shaped policy and governance during their tenures.

Duties and Responsibilities

The Vice President's duties encompass a range of roles and responsibilities, both within the executive branch and in the broader political sphere.

1. **Presiding Over the Senate:** The Vice President serves as the President of the Senate, with the authority to cast tie-breaking votes. This role is particularly significant in closely divided Senate chambers, where the Vice President's vote can be pivotal in passing or blocking legislation. For instance, Vice President Kamala Harris cast tie-breaking votes on several key pieces of legislation during the 117th Congress.
2. **Succession and Emergency Roles:** The Vice President is first in the presidential line of succession, ready to assume the presidency in the event of the President's death, resignation, or removal from office. This role is critical for maintaining continuity of government. For example, Lyndon B. Johnson became President following John F. Kennedy's assassination in 1963, and Gerald Ford assumed the presidency after Richard Nixon's resignation in 1974.
3. **Advisory and Policy Roles:** Modern Vice Presidents often take on substantial advisory and policy roles, assisting the President in shaping and implementing domestic and foreign policy. They may lead special task forces, work on key legislative

priorities, and represent the administration in negotiations and diplomatic efforts. Vice President Al Gore, for example, played a key role in advocating for environmental policies and climate change initiatives during the Clinton administration.

4. **Diplomatic and Ceremonial Functions:** The Vice President often represents the administration at official ceremonies, state functions, and international events. This role involves diplomacy and public relations, as Vice Presidents engage with foreign leaders, participate in global summits, and bolster the country's international relationships.

Impact and Contributions

Vice Presidents have made significant contributions to American political history, influencing policy, shaping administration priorities, and serving as key players in major historical events.

1. **Policy Influence:** Vice Presidents have had a notable impact on various policy areas. For example, Vice President Joe Biden was instrumental in advocating for the Affordable Care Act and led efforts on foreign policy issues such as Ukraine and Iraq during the Obama administration. Similarly, Vice President Dick Cheney played a key role in shaping U.S. foreign policy and national security strategies during the George W. Bush administration.

2. **Political Legacy:** Many Vice Presidents have leveraged their experience to pursue further political ambitions. Several former Vice Presidents have gone on to become Presidents, including Martin Van Buren, Richard Nixon, and Lyndon B. Johnson.

Others have continued to influence politics through public service, writing, and advocacy.
3. **Historical Events:** Vice Presidents have been involved in major historical events that have shaped the nation. For instance, Vice President Spiro Agnew's resignation in 1973 led to the appointment of Gerald Ford as Vice President, who later became President. Similarly, Vice President Kamala Harris's election as the first female, first African American, and first South Asian Vice President marks a significant milestone in American history.

Challenges and Criticisms

Despite their important role, Vice Presidents often face challenges and criticisms, including issues related to their perceived relevance and influence.

1. **Limited Constitutional Power:** The Vice President's constitutional powers are limited compared to those of the President, leading to perceptions of the role as less influential. The Vice President's reliance on the President's agenda and priorities can sometimes limit their ability to assert an independent policy vision.
2. **Balancing Acts:** Vice Presidents must navigate the complexities of serving as both a key advisor to the President and a political figure in their own right. Balancing these dual roles can be challenging, particularly when there are differences in policy preferences or political strategies.
3. **Public Perception:** The Vice Presidency is often viewed through the lens of public perception and media portrayal. Vice Presidents may struggle with

maintaining visibility and influence while dealing with the expectations and scrutiny that come with the role.

Looking Ahead

As the role of Vice President continues to evolve, future Vice Presidents will face new opportunities and challenges in shaping American governance.

1. **Expanding Roles:** Future Vice Presidents may see their roles expand further, taking on additional responsibilities and influencing policy in new ways. The increasing complexity of global and domestic issues may lead to a greater emphasis on the Vice President's role in addressing key challenges.
2. **Innovative Leadership:** The evolving political landscape presents opportunities for Vice Presidents to demonstrate innovative leadership and contribute to shaping the future of American governance. Embracing new approaches and addressing emerging issues will be crucial for maximizing the impact of the Vice Presidency.
3. **Public Engagement:** Enhancing public engagement and communication will be important for future Vice Presidents to build support, address concerns, and effectively represent the administration. Leveraging technology and media platforms will be essential for connecting with citizens and advancing policy goals.

Chapter - 2

FIRST LADIES: INFLUENCE FROM THE WHITE HOUSE

The role of First Lady of the United States is both ceremonial and influential, serving as a key figure in the White House and American society. Although not an official government position, First Ladies have historically wielded considerable influence through their public engagements, advocacy efforts, and support of their husbands' administrations. This chapter explores the evolving role of First Ladies, their contributions to American society, and their impact on the presidency.

The Role and Evolution of the First Lady

The role of the First Lady has evolved significantly since

the early days of the Republic. From primarily social and ceremonial duties, the position has expanded to encompass a range of responsibilities and public roles.

1. **Early Days and Ceremonial Duties:** The role of the First Lady began as a largely ceremonial position, with responsibilities focused on hosting social events and representing the President in public functions. Martha Washington, the first First Lady, set a precedent for hosting receptions and dinners, and her role was primarily limited to supporting her husband's role as President.
2. **Increasing Public Engagement:** By the 19th and early 20th centuries, First Ladies began to take on more visible and active roles. For example, Julia Grant and Edith Roosevelt were known for their social contributions and reform efforts. The position of First Lady continued to evolve, with increased engagement in social causes and public advocacy.
3. **Modern Era and Expanded Influence:** In the latter half of the 20th century and into the 21st century, First Ladies have taken on more substantial roles, using their platforms to advocate for various causes, influence public policy, and engage in significant social and political issues. Figures like Eleanor Roosevelt, Jacqueline Kennedy, and Michelle Obama have transformed the role into a position of active leadership and public influence.

Notable First Ladies and Their Contributions

Several First Ladies have made significant contributions through their advocacy, public initiatives, and influence on American society.

1. Eleanor Roosevelt (1933-1945):

- Advocacy for Human Rights: Eleanor Roosevelt was a transformative First Lady, deeply involved in social reform and human rights. She played a key role in advocating for the Universal Declaration of Human Rights, serving as the chair of the United Nations Commission on Human Rights.
- Social Reforms: Roosevelt championed numerous social causes, including civil rights, women's rights, and economic justice. Her work helped to redefine the role of First Lady and set new standards for public engagement and advocacy.

2. Jacqueline Kennedy (1961-1963):

- Cultural and Historical Preservation: Jacqueline Kennedy was known for her efforts to preserve and promote American culture and history. Her work in restoring the White House and promoting American arts and architecture left a lasting legacy.
- Public Image and Style: Kennedy's sense of style and public grace contributed to her popularity and influence. Her efforts in enhancing the White House's public image helped to elevate the role of the First Lady.

3. Hillary Clinton (1993-2001):

- Healthcare Reform: As First Lady, Hillary Clinton was heavily involved in advocating for healthcare reform, leading the efforts to develop the Clinton Health Care Plan. Although the plan was not enacted, her work highlighted the First Lady's potential role in policy advocacy.
- Women's and Children's Issues: Clinton championed issues related to children's welfare, women's rights, and family support programs. Her work laid the foundation for future advocacy and demonstrated the First Lady's capacity to influence policy.

4. Michelle Obama (2009-2017):

- Healthy Eating and Nutrition: Michelle Obama launched the "Let's Move!" initiative to combat childhood obesity and promote healthier eating habits. The program aimed to improve nutrition standards and physical activity for children.
- Education and Support for Military Families: Obama also focused on education initiatives, supporting military families, and advocating for girls' education globally. Her work in these areas expanded the First Lady's role in addressing key societal issues.

The Impact of First Ladies on the Presidency

First Ladies have often used their position to support their husbands' administrations and contribute to the overall effectiveness of the presidency.

1. **Supporting Policy Initiatives:** First Ladies frequently support and promote their husbands' policy agendas. Their involvement can help build public support for initiatives and provide a platform for advocacy. For instance, Eleanor Roosevelt's advocacy for the New Deal programs helped to garner support and public engagement.
2. **Enhancing Public Image:** The First Lady's public image can influence the President's administration, shaping perceptions and garnering public support. The grace, poise, and personal initiatives of First Ladies often reflect positively on the President and the administration as a whole.
3. **Bridging Political and Social Gaps:** First Ladies often engage in activities that bridge political and social gaps, working to address diverse issues and connect with various communities. Their involvement in social causes and public service can foster unity and promote positive change.

Challenges and Criticisms

Despite their significant contributions, First Ladies often face challenges and criticisms related to their roles and public perceptions.

1. **Balancing Public and Private Lives:** First Ladies must navigate the challenges of maintaining a private life while fulfilling public duties. The intense media scrutiny and public expectations can impact their personal lives and roles within the White House.
2. **Perceptions of Influence:** The influence of First Ladies can be a source of debate. Critics may question

the appropriateness of their involvement in policy and public issues, while supporters argue that their advocacy is valuable and impactful.
3. **Shifting Expectations:** The role of First Lady has evolved, and expectations continue to shift. Modern First Ladies are often expected to take on more active and diverse roles, which can create pressures and challenges in balancing these expectations with traditional duties.

Chapter - 3

CAMPAIGN FINANCE AND LOBBYING

Campaign finance and lobbying are critical components of the American political system, influencing the way campaigns are funded, conducted, and regulated. This chapter provides a detailed examination of the mechanisms of campaign finance and lobbying, their impact on politics, and the ongoing debates surrounding these practices.

Campaign Finance: An Overview

Campaign finance refers to the raising and spending of money by political candidates, parties, and interest groups to influence elections. The system is complex and regulated by a series of laws and regulations designed to ensure transparency and limit undue influence.

1. **Historical Context And Regulation:**
    - Early Developments: In the early days of American politics, campaign finance was relatively unregulated, with candidates relying on personal wealth and local support. However, the growing influence of money in politics led to increased regulation.
    - Federal Election Campaign Act (FECA): Enacted in 1971 and amended in 1974, FECA established the Federal Election Commission (FEC) and set limits on individual contributions to candidates. It aimed to increase transparency and reduce corruption.
    - Buckley v. Valeo (1976): This Supreme Court decision ruled that limits on individual expenditures were unconstitutional, as they infringed on free speech. The ruling allowed for greater personal spending by candidates and led to the rise of Political Action Committees (PACs).

2. **Key Regulations And Supreme Court Decisions:**

- Bipartisan Campaign Reform Act (BCRA): Passed in 2002, BCRA sought to address issues of "soft money" (unregulated funds) and improve transparency. It prohibited national parties from accepting soft money donations and increased disclosure requirements.
- Citizens United v. FEC (2010): The Supreme Court's decision in this landmark case

allowed corporations and unions to spend unlimited amounts on political advertisements, fundamentally altering campaign finance dynamics. This ruling led to the creation of Super PACs, which can raise and spend unlimited funds independently of candidates.

3. Modern Campaign Finance Dynamics:

- <u>Super PACs and Dark Money:</u> Super PACs, formed after the Citizens United decision, can raise unlimited funds from individuals, corporations, and unions. They often engage in high-profile advertising campaigns. Dark money refers to funds from nonprofit organizations that do not have to disclose their donors, leading to concerns about transparency.
- <u>Election Spending:</u> In the 2020 election cycle, approximately $14.4 billion was spent on federal elections, including presidential, Senate, and House races. Super PACs and outside groups accounted for a significant portion of this spending, with groups like Priorities USA Action and the National Rifle Association spending millions on advertising and advocacy.

Lobbying: Influence and Impact

Lobbying involves efforts by individuals or organizations to influence government decisions and policy-making. Lobbyists represent a wide range of interests, from corporations and trade associations to non-profit organizations and advocacy groups.

1. **The Role of Lobbyists:**
    - Advocacy and Representation: Lobbyists advocate for specific policies or legislation on behalf of their clients or organizations. They provide expertise, draft legislation, and engage in discussions with lawmakers to promote their interests.
    - Legislative Influence: Lobbyists play a significant role in shaping legislation by providing information, mobilizing public opinion, and influencing the decision-making process. Their influence can be seen in various policy areas, including healthcare, finance, and environmental regulation.
2. **Regulation and Transparency:**
    - Lobbying Disclosure Act (LDA): Enacted in 1995, the LDA requires lobbyists to register and report their activities, including their clients, expenditures, and the issues they are lobbying on. This legislation aimed to increase transparency and reduce the potential for corruption.
    - Federal Regulation of Lobbying Act: First passed in 1946 and later updated, this act established the requirement for lobbyists to register and report their activities. It provided a framework for regulating lobbying practices and improving public awareness.
3. **Influence and Criticism:**
    - Impact on Policy: Lobbying can significantly impact policy outcomes, as organizations and interest groups leverage their resources and expertise to shape legislation. For example,

pharmaceutical companies spend millions on lobbying efforts to influence drug pricing and regulation.
- <u>Criticism and Reform Efforts:</u> Lobbying is often criticized for enabling special interests to exert undue influence on lawmakers and potentially undermining democratic processes. Reform efforts have focused on increasing transparency, reducing the influence of money in politics, and addressing conflicts of interest.

The Intersection of Campaign Finance and Lobbying

Campaign finance and lobbying are interconnected, as both systems involve the flow of money and influence in politics.

1. **Campaign Contributions and Lobbying:**
   - <u>Political Donations:</u> Lobbyists and interest groups often contribute to political campaigns, creating a link between financial support and access to lawmakers. These contributions can lead to perceptions of quid pro quo arrangements and influence-peddling.
   - <u>Legislative Influence:</u> Campaign donations from lobbyists or their clients can affect legislators' positions on issues and their responsiveness to lobbying efforts. This dynamic raises concerns about the potential for corruption and the prioritization of special interests over the public good.
2. **Revolving Door Phenomenon:**
   - <u>Transition from Public to Private Sector:</u>

The "revolving door" phenomenon refers to the movement of individuals between government positions and lobbying or advocacy roles. Former lawmakers or government officials often become lobbyists, leveraging their connections and knowledge to influence policy.
- Impact and Concerns: This practice can lead to concerns about conflicts of interest and the potential for individuals to use their public service experience for private gain. Efforts to address the revolving door include stricter regulations and cooling-off periods for former officials.

Case Studies and Examples

Examining specific case studies provides insights into the practical implications and impact of campaign finance and lobbying.

1. **The 2010 Citizens United Decision:**
   - Background: The Citizens United v. FEC decision allowed unlimited spending by corporations and unions on political advertising. This landmark ruling fundamentally changed campaign finance dynamics and led to the rise of Super PACs.

- Impact: The decision increased the influence of wealthy donors and special interest groups, leading to concerns about the concentration of political power and the undermining of democratic principles. The ruling has been criticized for contributing to the erosion of public trust in the electoral process.

2. **The Influence of the Pharmaceutical Industry:**
    - Background: The pharmaceutical industry is one of the largest spenders on lobbying and campaign contributions, aiming to influence drug policy, pricing, and regulation.
    - Impact: Pharmaceutical companies have successfully influenced legislation related to drug pricing and patent protection. Their lobbying efforts have contributed to the high cost of prescription drugs and sparked debates about the need for reform in the healthcare system.

Reform and Future Directions

Efforts to reform campaign finance and lobbying practices focus on enhancing transparency, reducing the influence of money, and improving the integrity of the political process.

1. **Campaign Finance Reform:**
    - Proposals and Initiatives: Proposals for campaign finance reform include increasing disclosure requirements, implementing public financing of campaigns, and limiting the influence of Super PACs and dark money. Organizations like Common Cause and the

Campaign Legal Center advocate for reforms to promote transparency and accountability.
- Legislative Efforts: Various legislative efforts, such as the For the People Act, aim to address campaign finance issues by enhancing disclosure, regulating Super PACs, and reducing the influence of special interests.

2. **Lobbying Reform:**
   - Transparency and Accountability: Reform efforts focus on improving transparency in lobbying activities, such as strengthening disclosure requirements and addressing the revolving door phenomenon. Measures like the Honest Leadership and Open Government Act aim to enhance accountability and reduce conflicts of interest.
   - Public Engagement: Increasing public awareness and engagement in lobbying practicescan contribute to greater scrutiny and reform efforts. Advocacy organizations and media investigations play a role in highlighting issues and promoting changes in lobbying practices.

Chapter - 4

THE ELECTORAL MAP: SWING STATES AND BATTLEGROUNDS

The electoral map of the United States is a critical factor in presidential elections, with certain states playing a pivotal role in determining the outcome. These swing states, also known as battleground states, are characterized by their lack of predictable partisan allegiance, making them highly competitive and crucial for candidates to win. This chapter explores the significance of swing states, analyzes key battleground states, and examines the factors that influence their outcomes.

Understanding Swing States

and Battlegrounds

Swing states are states where both major political parties have similar levels of support among voters, leading to uncertain outcomes in elections. These states are vital for presidential candidates as winning them can significantly impact the overall result of the election.

1. **Definition and Importance:**
    - <u>Swing States:</u> Also known as battleground states, these are states where no single party has a clear majority of support. Their unpredictability makes them the focus of intense campaigning and advertising.
    - <u>Electoral Votes:</u> Each state has a certain number of electoral votes based on its population. Swing states often have a substantial number of electoral votes, making them especially important in close elections. For example, Florida (29 electoral votes) and Pennsylvania (19 electoral votes) are crucial due to their large number of electoral votes.
2. **Historical Context:**
    - <u>Early Elections:</u> In early American elections, the electoral map was less fluid, with fewer states considered battlegrounds. Over time, demographic and political shifts have increased the number of competitive states.
    - <u>Modern Trends:</u> The rise of closely contested states can be attributed to demographic changes, shifts in party alignment, and varying political priorities. The 2000 and 2016 elections, for example, were both decided by narrow margins in a few key swing states.

Key Swing States in Recent Elections

Several states have been consistently identified as critical swing states due to their competitive nature and significant electoral vote count.

1. **Florida:**
   - Electoral Votes: 29
   - Significance: Florida is a perennial battleground due to its diverse population, including significant Hispanic and senior voter blocks. In the 2000 presidential election, Florida's 29 electoral votes were decisive in determining George W. Bush's victory over Al Gore. In 2020, the state again played a crucial role in Donald Trump's re-election.
2. **Pennsylvania:**
   - Electoral Votes: 19
   - Significance: Pennsylvania's political landscape includes a mix of urban, suburban, and rural voters. The state was a key focus in the 2016 and 2020 elections, with Joe Biden winning it in 2020 to secure the presidency. Its electoral votes have historically been significant in close races.
3. **Ohio:**
   - Electoral Votes: 17
   - Significance: Ohio is known for its diverse electorate and swing nature, making it a key battleground. It has often been a bellwether state, reflecting the overall national mood. In 2008 and 2012, Barack Obama's victories in Ohio were crucial to his re-election, while in

2016, Donald Trump's win in Ohio helped secure his presidency.

4. **Michigan:**
   - Electoral Votes: 15
   - Significance: Michigan's economic and demographic changes have made it a key battleground. The state flipped from Obama in 2012 to Trump in 2016 and then back to Biden in 2020. Its working-class voters and union presence play a significant role in its electoral outcomes.
5. **Wisconsin:**
   - Electoral Votes: 10
   - Significance: Wisconsin has been a crucial swing state, with its outcomes often reflecting broader national trends. It was a decisive state in both the 2016 and 2020 elections, with Biden's narrow victory in Wisconsin contributing to his overall win.

Factors Influencing Swing States

Several factors contribute to the swing state status of certain regions, impacting how elections are contested and decided.

1. **Demographic Changes:**
   - Population Shifts: Demographic changes, such as the influx of new residents and shifts in voter composition, can alter the political landscape of a state. For instance, the growth of Hispanic populations in states like Arizona and Nevada

has made them increasingly competitive.
- Urban vs. Rural Divide: The divide between urban and rural areas often influences swing state dynamics, with urban areas typically leaning Democratic and rural areas leaning Republican. States with significant disparities between these regions, like Pennsylvania and Michigan, can be highly competitive.

2. **Economic Factors:**
   - Economic Issues: Economic conditions, such as unemployment rates, industrial decline, and economic recovery, can impact voter preferences in swing states. Economic issues often drive voters to prioritize candidates who address their concerns effectively.

3. **Political Campaign Strategies:**
   - Targeted Campaigning: Candidates and their campaigns invest heavily in swing states, focusing on targeted advertising, voter outreach, and mobilization efforts. Swing state voters receive a significant amount of campaign attention, including visits from candidates, advertisements, and grassroots efforts.
   - Polling and Data: Campaigns use extensive polling and data analytics to identify key issues and tailor their messages to swing state voters. This data-driven approach helps campaigns focus their resources on areas where they can make a difference.

Impact of Swing States on Elections

Swing states play a crucial role in determining the outcome of presidential elections, often serving as the deciding factor in close races.

1. **Election Outcomes:**
    - <u>Narrow Margins</u>: Swing states often decide elections by narrow margins, with small changes in voter behavior leading to significant shifts in the overall outcome. For example, in the 2020 election, Biden's wins in Pennsylvania, Michigan, and Wisconsin provided him with the necessary electoral votes to secure the presidency.
    - <u>Strategic Importance</u>: The strategic importance of swing states means that candidates focus their resources and campaign efforts on these areas, sometimes at the expense of other states. This focus can lead to intensified campaigning and high levels of voter engagement.
2. **Voter Turnout and Engagement:**
    - <u>Mobilization Efforts</u>: Campaigns invest heavily in mobilizing voters in swing states, often leading to higher voter turnout in these areas. Voter engagement efforts, such as rallies, advertisements, and grassroots campaigns, aim to increase participation and influence the outcome.
    - **Swing State Impact**: The increased attention and resources devoted to swing states can enhance voter awareness and participation, making these states a focal point of the electoral process.

Looking Ahead: Changes and Challenges

The landscape of swing states is continually evolving, influenced by demographic, political, and societal changes.

1. **Emerging Battlegrounds:**
   - New Swing States: As demographics and political preferences shift, new states may emerge as battlegrounds. States like Georgia and Arizona, which have become increasingly competitive, are examples of evolving political dynamics.
   - Long-Term Trends: Long-term trends, such as changing population patterns and evolving political attitudes, will continue to shape the electoral map and influence the status of swing states.
2. **Challenges and Reforms:**
   - Electoral Integrity: Ensuring the integrity of the electoral process in swing states is crucial for maintaining public confidence in elections. Addressing issues such as voter suppression, election security, and fair representation will be important for future elections.
   - Campaign Finance and Influence: The influence of money in swing state campaigning, including the role of Super PACs and dark money, presents challenges for transparency and equity in the electoral process. Reform efforts will need to address these issues to ensure a fair and democratic process.

Chapter - 5

THIRD-PARTY CANDIDATES: THE OUTSIDERS

Third-party candidates have played a significant role in American politics, often challenging the two-party dominance of the Democratic and Republican parties. While third-party candidates rarely win major offices, their campaigns can influence electoral outcomes, shift political discourse, and introduce new ideas into the political mainstream. This chapter explores the history, impact, and challenges of third-party candidates in U.S. elections.

The Historical Context of Third-Party Politics

Third-party politics in the United States has a

long history, characterized by various movements and candidates who sought to challenge the established two-party system.

1. **Early Third Parties:**
   - The Federalists and Democratic-Republicans: In the early years of the Republic, the Federalist and Democratic-Republican parties were the primary political factions. The rise of the Democratic-Republicans marked the beginning of the two-party system.
   - The Whigs and the Democrats: The Whig Party emerged in the 1830s as an opposition to the Democratic Party. The dissolution of the Whigs and the rise of the Republican Party in the 1850s further solidified the two-party system.
2. **Progressive Era and Reform Movements:**
   - The Populist Party: In the late 19th century, the Populist Party (People's Party) emerged, advocating for agrarian interests and economic reforms. The party's platform included demands for monetary reform, regulation of railroads, and direct election of Senators.
   - The Progressive Party: Formed by Theodore Roosevelt in 1912 after a split from the Republican Party, the Progressive Party focused on progressive reforms such as labor rights, environmental protection, and government regulation of business. Roosevelt's candidacy split the Republican vote and contributed to the election of Woodrow Wilson.
3. **Modern Third Parties:**
   - The Libertarian Party: Founded in 1971, the Libertarian Party advocates for limited

government, individual freedoms, and free-market principles. It has gained prominence in recent decades, with candidates like Gary Johnson running in the 2012 and 2016 elections.
- The Green Party: Established in the 1980s, the Green Party focuses on environmental issues, social justice, and nonviolence. Ralph Nader's candidacy in the 2000 election brought attention to the party and its platform.

Impact of Third-Party Candidates

While third-party candidates often face significant challenges in winning major offices, they can have a substantial impact on elections and political discourse.

1. **Electoral Influence:**
   - Spoiler Effect: Third-party candidates can influence election outcomes by drawing votes away from major party candidates. For example, Ralph Nader's candidacy in the 2000 presidential election is often cited as a factor in Al Gore's narrow loss to George W. Bush in Florida.
   - Vote Splitting: Third-party candidates can contribute to vote splitting, where the presence of multiple candidates from similar ideological backgrounds divides the vote. This can benefit candidates from opposing parties who may win with a plurality of votes.

2. **Shaping Political Discourse:**
    - <u>Introducing New Ideas:</u> Third-party candidates often bring new ideas and perspectives into political discourse, challenging the status quo and pushing major parties to address emerging issues. For example, the Green Party has emphasized environmental issues and climate change.
    - <u>Influencing Major Parties:</u> The success or prominence of third-party candidates can influence the platforms and policies of major parties. Major parties may adopt aspects of third-party platforms to appeal to their supporters and mitigate the impact of third-party challenges.

Challenges Faced by Third-Party Candidates

Third-party candidates face numerous obstacles that make it difficult for them to win major offices and gain widespread support.

1. **Electoral System:**
    - <u>First-Past-The-Post System:</u> The U.S. uses a winner-takes-all electoral system, where the candidate with the most votes wins, and there is no proportional representation. This system favors a two-party dominance and makes it challenging for third-party candidates to win significant offices.
    - <u>Ballot Access:</u> Third-party candidates

often face difficulties in gaining ballot access, requiring them to collect signatures and meet various state-specific requirements. This can be a significant barrier to entry for third-party campaigns.

2. **Funding and Resources:**
   - Limited Financial Resources: Third-party candidates typically have less access to campaign funding compared to major party candidates. This limits their ability to compete effectively in advertising, outreach, and media coverage.
   - Institutional Support: Major parties have established infrastructure, including party organizations, donor networks, and volunteer bases, that third-party candidates often lack. This disparity in resources can hinder third-party campaigns.

3. **Media Coverage:**
   - Limited Exposure: Third-party candidates often receive less media coverage compared to major party candidates, which impacts their visibility and ability to reach voters. Media bias towards the two major parties can limit the public's awareness of third-party options.
   - Debate Participation: Access to presidential debates is a significant challenge for third-party candidates. Debate participation is often restricted to candidates who meet certain polling thresholds or have significant support, further limiting the exposure of third-party candidates.

Notable Third-Party Candidates

Several third-party candidates have made notable impacts on U.S. politics, each contributing to the discourse in different ways.

1. **Ross Perot (1992, 1996):**
   - Background: Ross Perot, a billionaire businessman, ran as an independent candidate in 1992 and later as the Reform Party candidate in 1996. His campaign focused on fiscal responsibility, government reform, and trade issues.
   - Impact: Perot's candidacy in 1992 drew significant support and highlighted concerns about the national debt and trade policies. He received 19% of the popular vote, making it the most successful third-party bid since Theodore Roosevelt. His campaign also influenced subsequent discussions on budget deficits and trade agreements.
2. **Ralph Nader (2000, 2004):**
   - Background: Ralph Nader, a consumer advocate and Green Party candidate, ran for president in 2000 and 2004. His platform emphasized environmental protection, corporate accountability, and social justice.
   - Impact: Nader's 2000 candidacy is often credited with drawing votes away from Al Gore, contributing to George W. Bush's victory. Despite controversies, Nader's campaigns highlighted issues related to corporate influence

and environmental policy.
3. **Gary Johnson (2012, 2016):**
    - Background: Gary Johnson, the Libertarian Party candidate, ran for president in 2012 and 2016. His platform focused on limited government, individual liberties, and fiscal conservatism.
    - Impact: Johnson's candidacies increased the visibility of the Libertarian Party and garnered significant support. In 2016, he received nearly 4.5% of the popular vote, making it one of the highest percentages for a Libertarian candidate.

The Future of Third-Party Politics

The future of third-party politics in the U.S. remains uncertain, with ongoing debates about the potential for reform and the role of third-party candidates.

1. **Electoral Reforms:**
    - Ranked-Choice Voting: Some advocate for ranked-choice voting, which allows voters to rank candidates by preference. This system could provide more opportunities for third-party candidates by reducing the spoiler effect and encouraging diverse choices.
    - Proportional Representation: Proposals for proportional representation, which allocates seats based on the percentage of votes received, could also benefit third parties by providing a more equitable representation of voter preferences.
2. **Increased Engagement:**
    - Grassroots Efforts: Third parties may continue

to grow through grassroots efforts, social media, and digital campaigning. Increased engagement and innovative strategies can help third-party candidates overcome traditional barriers.
- <u>Public Support:</u> As political dissatisfaction with the two major parties grows, there may be increased support for third-party options. This shift could lead to greater opportunities for third-party candidates in future elections.

Chapter - 6

VOTER TURNOUT AND DEMOGRAPHICS

Voter turnout and demographics are critical factors in determining the outcomes of U.S. elections. Understanding who votes, how often, and why can provide valuable insights into the electoral process and its impact on election results. This chapter explores voter turnout trends, demographic influences, and the implications for American politics.

Voter Turnout: Trends and Statistics

Voter turnout refers to the percentage of eligible voters who actually cast a ballot in an election. It is a key indicator of political engagement and can vary widely depending on the type of election, the political climate, and other factors.

1. **Historical Trends:**
   - Early Elections: Voter turnout in early American elections was relatively high compared to modern standards. For example, turnout in the 1800 presidential election was around 80%, reflecting high political engagement during that period.
   - 20th Century Trends: Voter turnout fluctuated throughout the 20th century. The highest turnout in the 20th century occurred in the 1960s, driven by high levels of political activism and civil rights movements. For instance, the 1964 presidential election saw a turnout of 60.8% of eligible voters.
   - Recent Elections: In recent decades, voter turnout has varied significantly. The 2008 presidential election saw a turnout of 61.6%, while the 2016 election had a turnout of 60.1%. The 2020 election saw a notable increase, with approximately 66.8% of eligible voters participating, the highest rate since 1908.

2. **Turnout by Election Type:**
   - Presidential Elections: Presidential elections typically see higher voter turnout compared to midterm and local elections. For example, the 2020 presidential election had a turnout rate of 66.8%, compared to 50.3% for the 2018 midterm elections.
   - Midterm Elections: Midterm elections generally have lower turnout rates. The 2018

midterms saw the highest turnout for midterm elections in over a century, but still lower than presidential elections.
- Local and State Elections: Voter turnout in local and state elections often lags behind national elections. For example, municipal elections can have turnout rates as low as 20-30% in some areas.

Demographic Influences on Voting

Demographics play a crucial role in shaping voter turnout and electoral outcomes. Various factors, including age, race, gender, education, and income, influence voting behavior.

1. **Age:**
   - Youth Voters: Younger voters (18-29) have historically had lower turnout rates compared to older age groups. In the 2020 election, 50% of eligible voters aged 18-29 participated, up from 45% in 2016.
   - Senior Voters: Older voters (65 and older) tend to have higher turnout rates. In 2020, 71% of voters aged 65 and older cast ballots, reflecting their strong political engagement.
2. **Race and Ethnicity:**
   - White Voters: White voters have consistently had higher turnout rates compared to minority groups. In 2020, 68% of white voters participated in the election.
   - African American Voters: African American voter turnout has increased significantly over

the decades. In 2020, approximately 60% of eligible African American voters cast ballots, reflecting strong engagement in the electoral process.
- Hispanic Voters: Hispanic voter turnout has historically been lower than that of white and African American voters. In 2020, about 53% of eligible Hispanic voters participated, showing an upward trend in recent elections.

3. **Gender:**
   - Female Voters: Women have generally had higher voter turnout rates than men. In the 2020 election, 67% of eligible female voters participated compared to 65% of male voters.
   - Male Voters: Male voter turnout has been slightly lower than female turnout in recent years, although the gap has narrowed in some elections.

4. **Education:**
   - Higher Education: Voters with higher levels of education are more likely to vote. In 2020, 78% of college graduates participated in the election, compared to 47% of those with only a high school diploma.
   - Educational Attainment: Educational attainment influences political awareness and engagement, with more educated voters being more likely to participate in elections.

5. **Income:**
   - Higher Income: Higher-income individuals tend to have higher turnout rates. In 2020, 74% of voters with incomes above $100,000 participated in the election, compared to 50% of

those with incomes below $30,000.
- Economic Factors: Economic stability and access to resources can affect an individual's ability to vote, with higher-income individuals generally having more access to voting resources.

Implications for American Politics

Voter turnout and demographics have significant implications for American politics, affecting electoral outcomes, policy decisions, and political representation.

1. **Electoral Outcomes:**
   - Swing States: Demographic changes in swing states can influence election results. For example, the increasing Hispanic population in states like Florida and Arizona has made these states more competitive.
   - Shifts in Voting Patterns: Changes in demographic patterns can lead to shifts in voting patterns and party support. For instance, the growing youth vote and increasing diversity in the electorate have impacted recent election results.
2. **Policy Decisions:**
   - Representation: Voter turnout affects political representation, with higher turnout leading to more representative outcomes. Low turnout among certain demographics can result in policies that do not fully reflect the preferences of the entire population.
   - Issue Prioritization: Demographic groups with higher turnout rates can influence which issues

are prioritized by candidates and policymakers. For example, high turnout among older voters can lead to a focus on issues such as Social Security and healthcare.
3. **Political Engagement:**
    o <u>Mobilization Efforts</u>: Understanding voter demographics helps campaigns target their mobilization efforts effectively. For example, campaigns may focus on increasing turnout among young voters or minority communities.
    o <u>Voter Education</u>: Increasing voter education and outreach efforts can help improve turnout rates and ensure that all demographic groups are represented in the electoral process.

Challenges and Future Trends

Several challenges and future trends impact voter turnout and demographics in American politics.
1. **Voter Suppression:**
    o <u>Barriers to Voting</u>: Voter suppression tactics, such as restrictive voter ID laws and purging of voter rolls, can disproportionately affect marginalized communities and lower turnout rates.
    o <u>Legal and Advocacy Efforts</u>: Addressing voter suppression requires legal and advocacy efforts

to protect voting rights and ensure equitable access to the electoral process.

2. **Technological Changes:**
   - <u>Online Voting</u>: The potential for online voting could increase accessibility and turnout, although it also raises concerns about security and privacy.
   - <u>Digital Campaigning</u>: Digital campaigning and social media play an increasingly significant role in engaging voters and influencing turnout. Campaigns use digital platforms to reach and mobilize voters effectively.

3. **Demographic Shifts:**
   - <u>Increasing Diversity:</u> The growing diversity of the electorate presents both opportunities and challenges for political engagement. Understanding and addressing the needs and preferences of a diverse population will be crucial for future elections.
   - <u>Generational Changes:</u> The political attitudes and behaviors of younger generations will continue to shape the electoral landscape. Engaging with younger voters and addressing their concerns will be important for future political success.

TIMELINE OF US ELECTIONS

The Founding Era (1787-1800):

- **1787:** The Constitutional Convention in Philadelphia leads to the creation of the U.S. Constitution and the Electoral College system. This foundational period establishes the framework for the U.S. presidential elections.
- **1789:** George Washington is elected as the first President of the United States with John Adams as Vice President. Washington's unanimous election sets a precedent for future presidents.

The 19th Century (1800-1900):

- **1824:** The contentious election of John Quincy Adams over Andrew Jackson, despite Jackson's popular vote win, is marred by allegations of a "corrupt bargain."
- **1860:** Abraham Lincoln's election as President underscores the deepening divide over slavery, leading to the secession of Southern states and the onset of the Civil War.
- **1864:** Lincoln's re-election amid the ongoing Civil War signifies continued support for Union

preservation and the fight against Confederate forces.

Early to Mid-20th Century (1932-1964):

- **1932:** Franklin D. Roosevelt's election during the Great Depression marks the beginning of the New Deal era, focusing on economic recovery and social reforms.
- **1960:** The election of John F. Kennedy brings a new era of youthful optimism and international diplomacy, notable for the first-ever televised debates.

Late 20th Century to Early 21st Century (1972-2020):

- **1972:** Richard Nixon's victory is overshadowed by the Watergate scandal, which eventually leads to Nixon's resignation in 1974.
- **1980:** Ronald Reagan's election represents a shift toward conservative policies and economic reforms, emphasizing tax cuts and military expansion.
- **1992:** Bill Clinton's victory amid economic concerns and Ross Perot's third-party candidacy brings attention to fiscal policy and economic reforms.
- **2000:** The election between George W. Bush and Al Gore is one of the closest and most disputed in U.S. history, with the outcome decided by a narrow margin in Florida.
- **2008:** Barack Obama's historic election as the first African American President signifies

a transformative moment in U.S. politics, focusing on change and reform.
- **2016:** Donald Trump's victory over Hillary Clinton signifies a significant shift in American politics, with deep divisions and a focus on populist and nationalist sentiments.
- **2020:** Joe Biden's election amidst the COVID-19 pandemic and high voter turnout underscores the high stakes of pandemic management and socio-political issues.

UNKNOWN FACTS ABOUT US ELECTIONS

- **First Election with a Popular Vote:** The first U.S. presidential election in 1789 did not have a popular vote. George Washington was elected unanimously by the Electoral College.
- **Longest Presidential Campaign:** The 1828 presidential campaign between Andrew Jackson and John Quincy Adams is often cited as the longest, beginning shortly after the 1824 election.
- **Only President to Resign:** Richard Nixon is the only U.S. president to have resigned from office. He stepped down in 1974 amid the Watergate scandal.
- **First Female Presidential Candidate:** Victoria Woodhull was the first woman to run for President of the United States in 1872. She was nominated by the Equal Rights Party.
- **The "Whig Party" Origin:** The Whig Party, which existed in the 1830s and 1840s, was

named after the British Whig Party and was founded in opposition to Andrew Jackson's policies.
- **Electoral College Misconception:** In some states, electors are not legally bound to vote according to their state's popular vote. These are known as "faithless electors," though their number is very small.
- **Unique Voting Machines:** In the 1960 presidential election, voting machines in some areas were mechanical devices that used levers and dials rather than electronic ballots.
- **The "Magic Number":** The "magic number" to win the U.S. presidency is 270 electoral votes. This number represents a majority of the 538 total electoral votes.
- **First Black Senator:** Hiram Revels was the first African American to serve in the U.S. Senate, representing Mississippi from 1870 to 1871.
- **Historical Voter Turnout:** The highest voter turnout in U.S. history was in the 1864 presidential election, when about 80% of eligible voters participated, largely due to the Civil War.
- **Popular Vote vs. Electoral Vote:** In the 1824 election, John Quincy Adams won the presidency despite losing the popular vote to Andrew Jackson, due to the decision of the House of Representatives.
- **The "Third-Party Effect":** Ross Perot's 1992 presidential campaign is believed to have

influenced the outcome of the election, potentially costing George H.W. Bush his second term.
- **Early Voting:** Absentee voting was used in the early U.S. elections, but it was primarily for military personnel and those unable to travel to polling stations.
- **First Televised Debate:** The first presidential debate on television took place in 1960 between John F. Kennedy and Richard Nixon, and it significantly impacted the election.
- **"Spoiled" Ballots:** In the 2000 Florida recount, "hanging chads" (incomplete punch card ballots) became infamous and led to a Supreme Court decision that decided the election outcome.
- **Electoral Vote Allocation:** Maine and Nebraska are unique among U.S. states because they use a proportional method to allocate their electoral votes, unlike the winner-takes-all approach used by most states.
- **Dead Elector Problem:** In the 1872 election, Democratic candidate Horace Greeley passed away before the Electoral College met. Some electors voted for him anyway, creating a unique situation.
- **The Electoral College's Influence:** The Electoral College system was originally designed to prevent direct popular election of the president, reflecting the founders' concerns about direct democracy.

- **First Latino Senator:** The first Latino U.S. Senator was Octaviano Larrazolo, who served New Mexico from 1928 to 1930.
- **Change in Voting Age:** The 26th Amendment, passed in 1971, lowered the voting age from 21 to 18, following the argument that if 18-year-olds could be drafted for war, they should be able to vote.
- **"Only Man to Be Elected Four Times":** Franklin D. Roosevelt is the only U.S. president to be elected to four terms. The 22nd Amendment, passed in 1951, limits presidents to two terms.
- **Unique 1968 Convention:** The 1968 Democratic National Convention in Chicago was marked by widespread protests and riots, influencing the party's platform and subsequent political dynamics.
- **Unusual Vice Presidential Candidate:** Richard Mentor Johnson, vice president under Martin Van Buren, is known for being the first VP to be elected without a running mate, as he was elected separately by the Senate.
- **Contested Primary:** In 1980, Ronald Reagan and George H.W. Bush battled intensely for the Republican nomination, with Bush's "voodoo economics" criticism of Reagan's economic policies becoming well-known.
- **First Openly Gay Candidate**: In 1974, Kathy Kozachenko was the first openly gay person elected to public office in the U.S., serving on the Ann Arbor, Michigan City Council.

- **No Party Affiliation:** In some elections, independent or third-party candidates have managed to win significant offices despite the dominance of the two major parties, such as Jesse Ventura's gubernatorial win in Minnesota.
- **Women Voting Rights:** The first U.S. presidential election in which women could vote nationwide was in 1920, following the passage of the 19th Amendment.
- **Unique Voting Locations:** In some areas, voting booths were historically set up in unusual places, including schools, churches, and even bars, to maximize accessibility.
- **The "Brooks Brothers Riot":** During the 2000 election recount in Florida, a group of Republican operatives staged a demonstration at the Miami-Dade County election office, which became known as the "Brooks Brothers Riot."
- **Famous "Caucus" Origin:** The term "caucus" originated from the early American colonial period and was used to describe meetings of political leaders to discuss strategies and candidate nominations.

Thankyou for reading!

Printed in Great Britain
by Amazon